SUCKERPUNCHED

A woman's experiences as a log scaler

*Lois Wood
Edgewood B.C.*

Written by
LOIS WOOD

 FriesenPress

Suite 300 - 990 Fort St
Victoria, BC, V8V 3K2
Canada

www.friesenpress.com

Copyright © 2021 by Lois Wood
First Edition — 2021

All rights reserved.

No part of this publication may be reproduced in any form, or by any means, electronic or mechanical, including photocopying, recording, or any information browsing, storage, or retrieval system, without permission in writing from FriesenPress.

ISBN
978-1-5255-9341-3 (Hardcover)
978-1-5255-9340-6 (Paperback)
978-1-5255-9342-0 (eBook)

1. Biography & Autobiography, Personal Memoirs

Distributed to the trade by The Ingram Book Company

AUTHOR'S NOTE

I present an understanding of log scaling with the fun and challenges I experienced.

I unfairly lost my health and career, but my legacy and the account of my log scaling remains.

I maintained records over decades with no future purpose in mind until countless people encouraged me to make a brave leap to share a rare book of log scaling experiences and commended my tenacity in adversity. The preparation of this book was challenging when confronting painful memories but rewarding when revisiting happier times.

My book has not been severely edited or rewritten and therefore has natural and unintended shortcomings. The content was compiled from journals and was not changed sufficiently to 'flow' in a true literary sense. This is my story in my words.

My artwork and photos are unaltered originals.

Part 1 explains log scaling and presents my experiences. Entries are not entered in chronological order; calendar dates are shown since, e.g., snow in August was an unusual event.

Part 2 is life with brain trauma. At times, I was unable to write, and memories fail me. This part of my life would have been nearly impossible to write without diaries. The bare-bones entries have not been altered. This section is presented in chronological order over a period of about one year.

It covers a violent assault, PTSD, injustices by employers, WorkSafe compensation, a brief return to work and subsequent wrongful dismissal.

I have met countless victims of workplace injuries, injustices and livelong disabilities. The accounts of fatalities are heart wrenching. The hardships and injustices dealt me will show the necessity to comply with safety and labor laws.

> *When wealth is lost, nothing is lost.*
> *When health is lost, something is lost.*
> *When character is lost, all is lost. (Author unknown)*

TABLE OF CONTENTS

III	AUTHOR'S NOTE
VII	INTRODUCTION

1	**PART 1: Log Scaling Explanation and Experiences**
3	MAP OF WEIGH SCALE LOCATIONS
5	MY BACKGROUND
9	LOG SCALING EXPLAINED — BRIEFLY
17	SCALING BEFORE COMPUTERS
21	CHECK SCALING
23	SCALING PROCEDURES
35	LOADER OPERATORS
49	MEMORABLE TRUCKS
65	LOG SCALERS
69	PICK YOUR RUT CAREFULLY — YOU'LL BE IN IT FOR THE NEXT 80 KM
75	QUALITY CONTROL
79	SUPERVISORS AND BOSSES
85	COMPUTERS ARE NOT INTELLIGENT. THEY ONLY THINK THEY ARE.
91	BETWEEN AND AFTER WORK
93	MANLY VS. LOIS
101	OUTHOUSES
103	PRESERVE WILDLIFE… PICKLE A SQUIRREL
111	RADIO — WHERE ARE YOU?
117	ODDS AND ENDS
127	ON REFLECTION

129	**PART 2: A Year in the Life of a Victim of Workplace Violence and Post-Traumatic Stress Disorder As Recorded in my Journals**
131	FRIDAY, SEPTEMBER 6: THE ASSAULT
135	FRIDAY SEPTEMBER 15: COMPANY DECISION ON VIOLENCE

140	POST-TRAUMATIC STRESS DISORDER
149	OCTOBER 4: WHY DOES BOSS NOT BELIEVE ME?
157	OCTOBER 30: OCTOPUS OPEN UNTIL BREAKUP... FIVE MONTHS
162	DECEMBER 11: FIRST MEETING WITH BOSS SINCE ASSAULT
171	MARCH 8: PROPOSED RESTRICTED CONTACT SCALE PROCEDURE
178	MAY 7: NEEDLES SCALES
182	OCTOBER 1: RENATA
184	OCTOBER 5: WORD THAT I AM HISTORY
185	MY FIRST MEETING WITH EMPLOYERS AND SLUGGER'S' EMPLOYERS
195	**PART 3: Searching for Truth and Justice**
197	SEARCHING FOR TRUTH AND JUSTICE
197	GOVERNMENT OFFERED FUNDING FOR WORKERS TO EXIT FORESTRY
197	PREPARING FOR COURT
198	TRUTH AND JUSTICE FINALLY HAPPEN? FIRST SETTLEMENT CONFERENCE
199	THE SECOND SETTLEMENT HEARING
199	THE THIRD SETTLEMENT HEARING
199	TRIAL
201	FINANCIAL PENALTY
202	IS THIS A LOSS OR A WIN?
202	IN SUMMARY

INTRODUCTION

Tucked away in a closet was an accumulation of jokes, diaries and memories from my career in forestry and log scaling. Rediscovering this at a low part of my life when I felt so much had been unjustly and deliberately taken from me was, at first, more unbearable pain. Somehow, I found the strength to begin reading and realized the value before committing the entirety to ashes. I rediscovered laughter. Not all could be taken from me; my legacy as a scaler remains, as do the memories of sharing laughter.

> *'The most utterly lost of all days, is that in which you have not once laughed.'*
> Sebastion Roch Nicolas Chamfort

> *'Work is one of the most fundamental aspects in a person's life, providing the individual with a means of support and, as importantly, a contributory role in society. A person's employment is an essential component of his or her sense of identity, self-worth and emotional well-being.'*
> Supreme Court of Canada – McKinley v B.C. Tel (Tevlin Gleadle – counsel)

THE COMPILATION

The log scaling experiences in Part 1 are not entered in exact chronological order. Most are from the years 1979 through 2008. Not all specific years are recorded and I have loosely grouped different subjects.

I chose to print my original notes, diaries and cartoons without changing, however, some explanations were added when necessary. I avoided full names and, in most instances, used pseudonyms.

The B.C. Government changed the designation of the forestry branch several times from Forest Service to Ministry of Forests and currently it is Ministry of Forests, Lands and Natural Resources. Throughout these memoirs, I have consistently, but at times somewhat inaccurately, referred to the B.C. Government branch as the Forest Service.

During my years as a log scaler, I recorded the sad, funny and absurd, and years later realize it is a momentous chronicle to share. Enjoy....

PART 1
Log Scaling Explanation and Experiences

The wall shows part of our filing system at Needles scales. The pink copies of weigh slips were sorted by contractor and given to them at month end. The original (white) copies were sorted: pre-scaled loads for the timber and pulp companies and scaled loads for the Forest Service month end. The scales finally had (outdated but useable) radios for communicating with truckers and loader operators. A laptop computer printed out daily and month-end reports and could send data electronically to the main office.

SAMPLE LOAD SPREAD FOR SCALING
RENATA SCALES

MAP OF WEIGH SCALE LOCATIONS

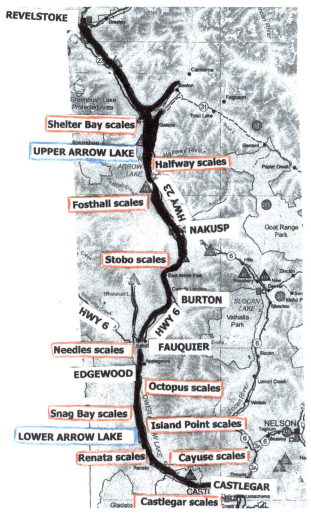

Tugboats towed booms of logs from nine scale sites to sawmill and pulp mills at Castlegar. The Tree Farm License was issued to the timber company by the Forest Service (B.C. Government) for logging and covered much of this area.

MY BACKGROUND

I spent two years at college studying Forestry Technology. Initially, my work was mainly in silviculture (mapping areas for tree planting, mapping areas that had naturally reseeded and studying areas scheduled to be logged). Kathy, Susan and I were among the first women to study forestry. I reflect now how little I appreciated the efforts made by Tor, our first Forest Service supervisor. He attempted to prove how women, although we were really just teenagers, could break into a male dominated world as we were believed to be the first female field crew outside of tree planters in the district.

The East Kootenays were devastated by forest fires in the 1920s. The 1970s Forest Service forest cover maps were sorely outdated. Large areas on the maps were labeled as having no natural tree regeneration and our job was to inspect and update these. Lodgepole pine requires fire to open cones to seed a new forest, growing at times as 'thick as hair on a dog's back', yet outdated records showed barren land. We mapped areas using a Silva compass and a 'chain' (a steel measuring tape 2 chains, or 132 feet, in length). Back at our camp or office, our recorded notes were mapped on paper with the aid of a protractor, ruler and pencil.

We were issued two-wheel drive trucks but had Honda 70 mini-bikes to access the rough roads and trails.

During our first year, we were the only persons staying in the Flathead Valley in the southeast corner of B.C. We had no radio communication outside the isolated area but survived silly escapades like trying unsuccessfully to drive across a boulder-filled creek that we fortunately were able to back out of. Our pickup didn't survive without incident and when the brakes failed, we drove it to Fernie for repairs. Without radio communication, we three donned our hard hats and bravely, or mindlessly, set off down a road chock-full of logging trucks. We met a logging truck, swerved into the ditch and carried on. Kathy and Susan frantically made a sign 'NO BRAKES' and held it up against the windshield to warn the next trucker we met. The traffic then parted miraculously like the Red Sea and we made it to the garage.

Tor patiently taught us not only Forest Service requirements but also bush skills. We learned survival expertise and off-road driving. Roped to Tor on the bank of a river, we practiced crossing the torrent using a thin pole for stability. Tor had a grandiose plan to access an old burned area that had no road access; Kathy, Susan and I were to secure poles on each side of our mini-bikes, rest the pole ends on our shoulders, and partner up to carry our bikes across the Wigwam River. Once across the river, we would travel to the worksite with enough gear to sustain us for a long period. Tor ultimately shelved that idea and chose instead to treat us to a helicopter flight.

I was hired during forest fire season in various capabilities. I also planted trees and cleared brush on planted sites.

I never planned to spend decades log scaling but that was the direction my career took.

Expose yourself to scaling.

I was conscripted from weigh scales by the Forest Service to work as a first aid attendant with fire fighters on a steep rocky slope on Mount St. Leon where loose rocks were easily and <u>unintentionally</u> dislodged. This caricature was humor in the face of danger. 'Compo' is slang for worker's compensation.

A LARGE WHITE PINE LOG. NOTE THE USUAL SCALE STICK WAS TOO SHORT TO MEASURE DIAMETERS. THE ROTTEN BUTT MAY SEEM LIKE THE LOG WAS PULP (NOT SAWLOG QUALITY). ACTUALLY, AFTER 3 METERS LENGTH, THE LOG WAS TOTALLY SOUND. AND WAS VERY VALUABLE. [STEVE WOOD PHOTO]

LOG SCALING EXPLAINED - BRIEFLY

In the Selkirk Mountains of southern British Columbia, the Columbia River between Revelstoke and Castlegar widens to become the Arrow Lakes. A Crown owned Tree Farm License, managed by a timber company, covers a vast area.

Locally, truckloads of logs are scaled, dumped in the lake and towed with tugboats to the Castlegar sawmill and pulp mill.

The logs are scaled first so the volume and quality can be calculated, from which the Forest Service collects stumpage fees and maintains an inventory of our forests. The logging contractors and the timber sellers are paid using the scaled volume. The local truckers are usually paid by the tonne hauled and by the allotted cycle time (a monetary rate for the distance traveled).

As a scaler, honesty is paramount because an error could mean unfair losses or returns (gains) to anyone involved in the timber harvesting or sale.

Forest Service check scalers measure my previously scaled load to ensure it meets stringent government accuracy requirements.

LOIS WOOD

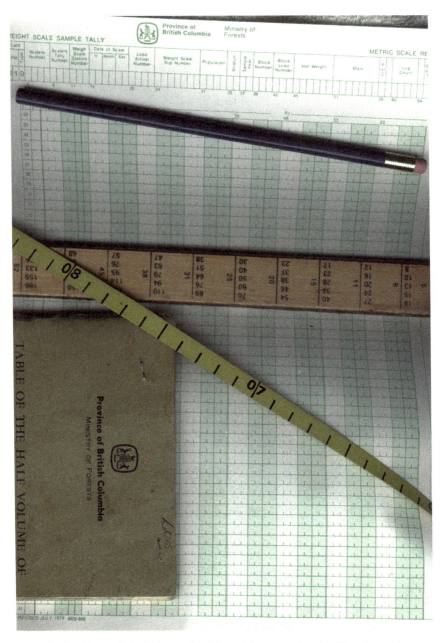

Tools of the trade include a scale stick used for measuring log diameters and referencing volumes of logs and defects (e.g. rot deductions), a tape for measuring log lengths, a pencil and data record sheet. Handheld computers eliminated the need for pen and paper and manually summarizing data.

Fig. 15 18.3 5
All retired scalers reminisce on how being a scaler is a wondrous thing.... Working in the lovely outdoors and fresh air and not in an office!

In 1988, I presented a retiring Forest Service check scaler with a collection of cartoons.

Above: All retired scalers reminisce on how being a scaler is a wondrous thing, working in the lovely outdoors and fresh air, and not in an office.

Following: 'Loader-man communication'

Chapter 12   Section 88-3
Loaderman communication

A scaler must be able to communicate with the loaderman. Hand signals should be learned.

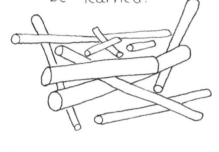 

Fig. 12 88.3 1
(Metric) "I believe you did not spread this load of logs very well."

Fig. 12 88.3 2
(Pre-metric - in event loaderman is not fully conversant in Metric)
"I believe, sir, that you just drove your loader into my pick-up."

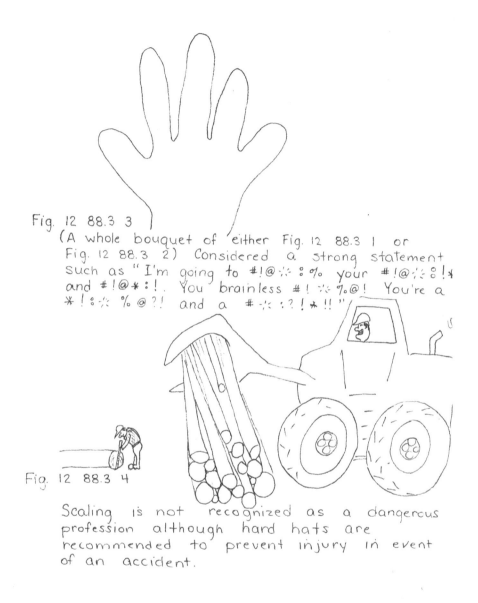

Fig. 12 88.3 3
(A whole bouquet of either Fig. 12 88.3 1 or Fig. 12 88.3 2) Considered a strong statement such as "I'm going to #!@☆:% your #!@☆:º!☆ and #!@*:!. You brainless #!☆%@! You're a *!:☆%@?! and a #☆:?!*!!"

Fig. 12 88.3 4

Scaling is not recognized as a dangerous profession although hard hats are recommended to prevent injury in event of an accident.

Weigh scales eliminate the need to measure every individual log. Random loads, 'sample loads', are chosen to calculate and apply a numerical factor to loads within that species and log quality category to establish a weigh/volume ratio. For example, cedar may have a ratio of 1.44 so a 30,000 Kg. load would have a cubic meter volume of 43.2 (30,000 x 1.44). Hemlock is a heavy wood and a 30,000 Kg. load may be 30 cubic meters.

The Needles scale office was more commonly called 'scale shack.' Later the scales were moved slightly north to accommodate a longer scale platform.

A required minimum number of samples in each category is randomly selected; fir sawlogs may require one sample per 70 loads; a less common load may necessitate sampling every load. The sample loads are hand scaled: the truck is unloaded, and a loader spreads the logs, so each log is visible to the scaler who then measures lengths and diameters of each log in the load to determine the volume. Rot must be deducted. The log is also graded as to the quality and quantity of potential lumber. If a log cannot make lumber, it is destined for the pulp mill.

At times, the number of samples randomly chosen by the computer can overtax the scaler and the loader operators. Measuring a few logs at a time, often at the bottom of a hill, with continual interruptions to run up to weigh a logging truck is good exercise although not usually appreciated as such.

The sort-yard is a necessary area for spreading sample loads for hand scaling. Also, loads that have a mix of species are put in the sort-yard so the loaders can sort by species since the bundles of logs go directly from the water into the sawmill. The mill cuts one species at a time. Fir, therefore, cannot be in the same truckload of logs as hemlock.

'Yard trucks' haul the sorted loads from the sort-yard, across the scales and then dump them in the lake. These loads are weighed for company inventory only; the wood was initially scaled for Forest Service purposes.

A loaded logging truck arriving at the scales is weighed, information about the load is entered into the computer and he leaves to dump his load in the lake or sort-yard. When he returns to weigh out, the net weight of his load is calculated.

Some weigh scales are hectic and remote ones can be ridiculously slow. I weighed 97 loads of logs in a day as the sole scaler and preferred that to processing as few as 3 a day.

Scaling at Needles on a mild spring day. Logs were improperly spread with the ends overhanging a steep bank. When a cold wind howls along the lake and snow covers the logs, scaling has added challenges.

Workers are preparing to dump a sample load of spruce in the Needles sort-yard.

An empty truck returns to Snag Bay scales to weigh out. The empty (tare) weight is subtracted from his loaded weight to obtain the weight of the load of logs.

SCALING BEFORE COMPUTERS

I began scaling without computers. Trucks were weighed using a large balance beam. The top 'handle' was moved along the weight numbers until the end of the beam (off photo) balanced. Information for the load was written on carbon paper. The weigh slip was inserted in a slot and the weight printed by squeezing a handle on the lower side of balance beam.

Daily lists of all loads were written by pencil on Forest Service forms. One page was used for one stratum (species category) for each timber mark with the number of loads and the weights recorded. The daily entries then had to be summarized on quadruple carbon- copy forms for the month.

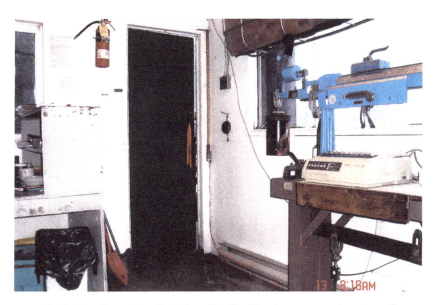

The balance beam is on the right at Needles. The door was merely a piece of plywood that blew open in the wind. A trucker gave me a rubber bungee cord to hold the door closed and stop snow from drifting inside. A scale stick, used for measuring log diameters, hangs from a nail to the right of the door.

LOIS WOOD

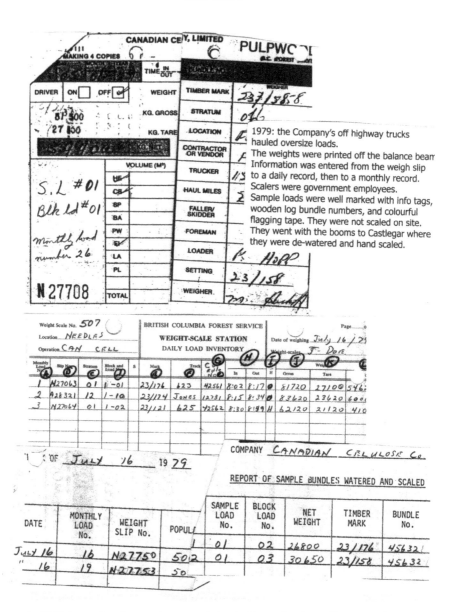

In 1979, I was given instructions to scale by the Forest Service scaling supervisor. Information on each load was recorded on a Daily Load Inventory form. Copies of the weigh scale load slip were distributed to the Forest Service, logging contractor and trucker. At that time, log scalers were government employees. B.C. Legislation later privatized log scaling and allowed logging companies to employ scalers.

One month I had weighed 1000 loads, which generated an impressive amount of paper. The weights and number of loads had to balance. Imagine my frustration when I had 999 loads on the summary and 1000 on another form. As I checked and rechecked all the paperwork, I became increasingly agitated but I persevered. Finally, the error was found; my boss had entered '1' load on a daily entry instead of the correct '2'.

At that time, scaling was done without the benefit of modern calculators. Math calculations were done by hand. We did have waterproof (somewhat!) paper. We had huge adding machines manually powered by pulling a lever down to print each entry. I borrowed a small battery powered calculator when I wrote my scaling exam. At that time, a good wage was $404.00 per month; the calculator cost $69.99. The Forest Service examiners were very impressed with the innovative technology, "Wouldn't they be handy to have!!!" Mine weighed about 15 pounds lighter than theirs!

THE AGE OF COMPUTERS

Fast forward to today: Electronics and telephones transfer data daily to all the company offices as well as the Forest Service offices. Sample loads are scaled using a handheld computer that can calculate rot deductions, print the data and transfer all the data electronically to the company and Forest Service offices.

When I arrived at work with trucks lined up waiting and arriving non-stop after that, I must have run on adrenalin. Every two or three minutes a truck can be weighed in loaded or out empty. When a loaded logging truck stops on the scales, the load must be inspected for species, log quality and presence of a timber mark showing the origin of the load. Methodically, I noted the truck name and number and the safety of the load (e.g. any overhanging logs).

Drivers gave me a load description slip listing the contractor, truck, timber mark and other pertinent information.

Information on the load is entered into a computer. Identifying tags are fastened to loads dumping in the lake and for sample loads. Some loads are marked with spray paint to assist the tug-boaters in sorting and booming species and pulp.

CHECK SCALING

Scalers are routinely checked by Forest Service 'check scalers'. The check scalers scale a load of logs and compare their results with the scalers'. There are stringent parameters. A scaled load can be cancelled and replaced by the check scalers' results if it exceeds 3% of the volume or value. Honest and correct scaling should be ensured.

This is a report from the Forest Service of a check scale. (Some information has been obscured here due to privacy concerns.) The original scale data by a scaler is compared to the random, unannounced check by the Forest Service check scaler. This reports the differences in load volume, stumpage value, number of logs recorded, grades, diameters and species. This report states 'Over a 12-month period, differences with check scales indicate your scale has a bias of 0.01 %.'

Check scalers are chain-sawing a log to see how far the rot extends to check the grade difference.

Loads of logs arriving at the weigh scales have to be stratified (categorized by quality, pulp or sawlogs, green or dry, and species). Assessing the load while on the truck could be a challenge.

Journal entries:

I stratified a mixed species load as less than 60% fir and more than 20% cedar. After hand scaling, I verified the load was 55% fir and 25% cedar with 20% hemlock.

I called a lodgepole load at least 40% dry and it scaled out as 42%.

SCALING PROCEDURES

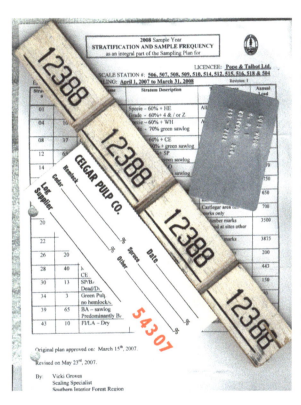

In the 1970s, wooden tags were nailed on the load ends with aluminum nails. In the 1990's, embossing machines for imprinting credit cards were re-purposed to create load information on aluminum tags and stapled to load corners. These were used in conjunction with coloured paper circles to denote pulp or size of the logs. (The sawmill had two sides: one for big logs, the other for small. A mixture of sizes was called 'bush run' and could be sawn in either section of the mill.)

Metal was detrimental to wood chip (pulp) quality, so these tags became obsolete. A system of writing information with indelible ink on coloured paper tags and stapled (minimal metal) to loads evolved.

Highway scales like Needles are challenging since truckers may have never tripped their stakes to release the load into the lake; some mill yards lift the entire load off. A new trucker received a brief orientation – radio channel frequency, directions to the lake or sort-yard, and load dumping procedures. With a growing lineup of trucks behind them, they are waved on with a hope and a prayer. Any problems dumping their loads caused chaos and unappreciated delays to other truckers.

A loader operator said I was the only scaler who enjoyed the challenge of the busiest scales. He said he felt the same adrenalin rush looking up the hill to see a never-ending line of truck lights and have everything run efficiently.

When Darwin, an accountant, phoned to inform me of an error I'd made, I apologized because I should have caught it myself. Darwin said, "You are doing more than half of all the loads (1500 in a month) in the Tree Farm License and I call you less than anyone for errors."

I do take pride in my work and put effort into it. There are scalers who never leave their desk to examine a load, and the subsequent errors are usually due to that. My employer offered to 'fix my sample' when the hand scale showed more dry pulp in a load than I had estimated. I emphatically said, "No." It is impossible to determine the exact nature of a load while it's on a truck. Of course, I'm not perfect!

I was continually humbled as I scaled. Loads and logs are not identical. A logging loader-man remembered me years later, even though he worked in the area only a few months. He said, "A loader operator can become very skilful at loading logs. They can place dry logs on the outside of the load and hope to hide green logs within. They write 'dry load' on their load advice slip, aware that the load is mainly green. I remember you; we could not get those past your inspection." I stood out because of my accuracy.

Many scalers were fooled because they never left their desk. Dry wood is lighter than green freshly harvested. Loads with the same weight have more volume of dry wood as compared to green.

A contractor paid by volume of timber harvested would benefit if a scaler stratified green logs as dry. Stumpage paid to the Government was often less by cubic meter (volume) for salvaging dead trees as opposed to harvesting live (green).

When the truck arrives at the dumpsite at the lake, the load is secured by 'wrapping' with cables. The truck's load binders are removed, the stakes on the lakeside of the load are released and the load slides down the ramp, or 'skids', into the lake. A push on the load from the loader is often required. The truck trailer is then loaded on the truck, piggy-back style.

A self–loading truck is leaving Needles scales. Trucks could haul to Needles on logging roads and bypassing a highway. Off-highway loads could exceed highway restrictions. Unique to this area was the enclosed seat to protect the operator from extreme weather as he loaded the truck, necessary at Anaheim Lake in the Cariboo/Chilcotin. 50,000 Kg. net weight in light wood like cedar required extra wide and extra high off-highway bunks to accommodate such a huge volume.

Snag Bay area hemlock can be deceptive. The butt and top of logs (top 3 photos) look deceptively sound with no rot. (Bottom 2 photos: The center of the log, at times 80% of the length, is worthless except as pulp. Sometimes rotten knots indicate rot, but these logs often had no indicators. Not until the logs were bucked (cut with a chain saw) was rot apparent. One bucker on a logging show said he'd never had such a tough time in 20 years after I had brought this to his attention. Sawing these logs for lumber would not have been profitable.

Snag Bay scales were ineffectively located for one season at the log dump by the lake. The loader could only use a short piece of the haul road to sort mixed loads and spread samples. The scales were moved back 3 kilometers from the lake to a sort-yard for the next season. Sadly, my chance to cool off in the lake was gone. The red display between the printers was our early electronic data entry computer. When not in use, it reverted to a clock. This one was goofy – e.g. 14:68 PO (11:20 AM). Prompts to enter data displayed as e.g. D%BV (contractor number). I had to remember the order entries were made. While dismantling the equipment at the end of the season, the problem was found to be electrical faults from the generator. Why I had to endure such unnecessary trials is beyond comprehension.

February 17- Needles

657 loads so far in February. Foggy, damp, muddy and I wonder how long work (roads) will last. Shoveled mud off scales on my own time before I went home.

February 21 – Needles

Our yard is giving out. Ray said he needed full power to go downhill with his load of logs.

October 31 – Needles

I stayed late to print out the month-end and glad of it even if it's on my own time. There's just no time during the day between trucks.

January 10 – Needles

93 loads today! Love it!

January 18 – Needles

I will hit 1000 loads so far this month by noon.

Octopus

Neil and Steve kept trying to light the propane heater in the scale shack but it kept going out. #@*&^% Finally Steve coiled up a big wad of paper and stuck it inside. Aha. We'd been trying to light a leak in the line, not the pilot light as we'd originally thought. Fortunately, there was no boom.

Snag Bay

A pole company asked me to send a notice to a logging crew:

'Could you please advise your bucker that 90-foot poles cannot be delivered as two 45 foot sections. If a landing visit is necessary to explain, please call Bud.'

Needles

A letter to the Forest Service explained why a load destined to be a hand scaled sample could not be unloaded:

'This load came up a sample. One loader was broken down. The second loader started picking off the load and broke a fork. The trucker could not trip his load on the left side to dump on the sample skids and the yard was too plugged to even put down temporary skids. It is a tri-axle truck so he could not have backed all the way up the hill to an alternate spot. The mixed loads waiting to dump were behind him and the tri-axle behind him couldn't back up anyways. He had waited two hours, so I allowed the sample load to dump in the lake. The next spruce stratum 12 load will be pulled for a replacement sample.

Shelter Bay news

Terry was telling me there is a three- hour wait to get through Shelter Bay scales. The trucks are backed up even onto the highway.

A female scaler there told me a trucker stepped out of his truck naked. He said it was hot out and he forgot he had no clothes on. Unbelievable, both the lack of clothes and her tolerance!

A self-loading logging truck left the scales at Needles and is driving through spring mud in the sort-yard to dump his load in the lake.

SUCKERPUNCHED

The trucker stopped to secure his load with cables prior to dumping it into the lake at the Octopus log dump.

Photos on left: Loading a truck on a logging site above Octopus scales
Right, top to bottom: Hauling in winter, Octopus sort-yard, Octopus log dump

This tug was used for sorting and booming logs of loads at Needles log dump. A larger tug is used to tow the booms to Castlegar.

UNDERSTANDING WEATHER STATIONS

Data records from weather stations during the summer determined the fire hazard of logging. Precipitation, temperatures and relative humidity were factors in implementing 'early shift' in which logging was permitted but only during hours of reduced fire risk. As the fire danger increased, logging activities were shut down. A spark from logging equipment could begin a wildfire.

Although weather stations could be close geographically, data could vary significantly, and some loggers had to cease logging while others continued to work.

Loggers believed they could advantageously choose a weather station to monitor to gain more time logging.

The cartoon offers ludicrous suggestions for rain recorded at a weather station during a sunny spell.

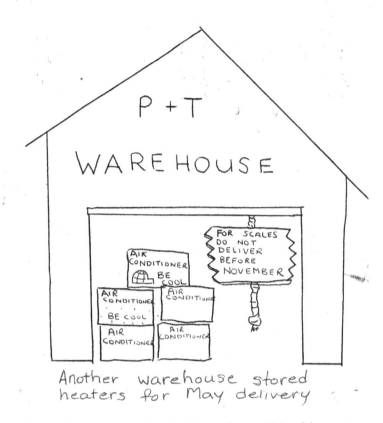

Another warehouse stored heaters for May delivery

Air conditioners were implemented due to the sensitivity of the operation of electronic equipment to heat and dust. The cartoon was inspired after enduring hot and dusty summers with no air conditioner.

May 1991 (Pre-air conditioners at scales) Vandals broke the big window at Needles at least twice; once by a five-gallon bucket thrown through it. A big sheet of plywood was put over it for a long spell making the shack dark and dreary. Finally, it was replaced by glass but the sun shining through the south-facing window made the computer hot causing it to malfunction. It was suggested I find a piece of plywood to put over the glass.

    Heaters (propane or electric) were available at my scales long after the cold arrived; One year it was November 27. I lit campfires to garner some warmth; fortunately, the sort-yard had lots of firewood! I wore a snowmobile suit all day.

December 22 – Snag Bay

Brrr. Very cold. Got to the scale shack and there was no propane. Brrr. Put on snowmobile suit. A two-liter bottle of water is frozen solid. Printer would not work, whirrrr, print one letter. Whirrrr, print second letter. Prrreett, whirrrr, uuhhh, print third letter.

NEEDLES LOADER FERRY + FAUQUIER IN BACKGROUND

LOADER OPERATORS

Loader operators came with different attitudes, ambitions and skill. The lack of any of the above became apparent when the workload increased.

Mixed species loads were sorted in the log yard before reloading on a truck and putting in the lake. Inadequate room to sort species was a common occurrence at logging sites.

In 2003, Ingersol Fire sent ash and burnt leaves and sticks into the Needles sort-yard.

Renata scale shack is to the left of photo. These logs are sample loads spread for hand scaling. Loads were dumped into the lake just past the yellow truck. Tugs had boomed bundles of logs.

Load hits water at Snag Bay log dump.

The sample yard at Stobo (Arrow Park) where some loads are spread for the scaler, some loads are decked for future scaling and some scaled loads are decked to reload destined for the lake. The last scaled load is to be left for the check scalers.

Some loader operators were not skillful at unloading a sample at Stobo (Arrow Park).

A yard truck is being loaded at the Snag Bay sort-yard. These logs came to the yard as mixed species or sample loads. The yard-truck load is weighed only for company inventory purposes; the wood was already scaled.

Snag Bay scales and sort-yard were 3 kilometers from the lake and water was rarely available to water down the dust. A loader-man claimed he could not see his loader forks for dust. (Photo had to be timed to show more than zero visibility.)

August 14 - Snag Bay

I gave a forester some photos of the dusty sort-yard and he agreed Seemore is working in awful conditions and there's enough work for another loader. He said there are three loaders at Halfway scales, but he does not know what they are doing.

October 2 - Snag Bay

A grow op was busted by police past the sort-yard. The Company should have seen the elaborate water system pumping water up Johnston Creek canyon. They cannot figure a way to water the dust in the sort-yard.

July 10 - Snag Bay

A trucker said when Dick A. was loading logs on a truck on a landing, they'd roll off the other side, the skidder would skid them around, so Dick could load them on the truck again. The logs would roll off, the skidder would skid them back around…..finally the skidder skidded them down the road to the next landing and a better loader operator.

The Needles beach trapped the loader in soft sand.

SNAG BAY UNEXPECTED EVENTS

I was scheduled for a medical procedure and asked my boss for the prior day off so I could take the pre-surgery medications at home, but he said I had to go to Snag Bay to open it for the season.

The loader operator and I heard a lot of talking on the radio. At first, the locations called were on Burrell Creek road where trucks hauled to Grand Forks. We were completely baffled when the road kilometers called over the radio were locations ever closer to us. Soon, a long line of trucks arrived at the scales with Celgar pulp. Those loads required different data not programmed into the Snag Bay computer, so every load had to be sent to the sort-yard. No loads could go to the lake to dump. I made my own computer registry to identify trucks. I sent a message to my supervisor, but he failed to acknowledge a critical problem. My printers were not even working right. I came in from scaling a load and a two-inch stack of weigh slips had gone through the printer. Over seventy sample loads had to be individually tagged and separated for hand scaling in the sort-yard. In addition, regular company sample loads and mixed sawlog loads continued to arrive for the sort-yard. The loader-man was tested to the maximum.

Despite the chaos, truckers were barely inconvenienced. I hoped in the final wrap-up, my records would not show loads to scale and none left in the yard. Or conversely, loads spread for me to scale of which I had no record.

We got through the ordeal with a perfect score.

As a scaler thrust into unforeseen circumstances and a potentially catastrophic data nightmare, I knew having an exceptional loader operator was a godsend that had averted disaster. Truckers appreciated his super-human effort.

FOSTHALL MISHAP

In November 2006, the loader-man and I traveled through deep snow to Fosthall scales. Immense walls of billowing snow engulfed our pickup as we forged ahead.

I set to work shoveling snow off the scales while the loader operator plowed the sort-yard and log dump. He then attempted to plow the haul road above the scales. By not having chains on all tires, he lost traction and slid to the brink of a precipitous cliff. A grader was called to the rescue and was able to attach a chain to the loader but as he tried to pull, the loader slid off the embankment. While the loader hung from a mere steel thread, a D8 Cat was low bedded to the rescue. It was a tense time for many hours waiting for the bulldozer but ended well. At 4:00 p.m. with the road now open for traffic, the first logging trucks weighed in.

When Mighty experienced a rare slow time operating the Snag Bay loader, he carved full size bears with a chain saw. He left one carved from a hemlock pulp log at the scales where it was an interesting display until it was taken and sold at the thief's yard sale.

SNAG BAY WIT

One day, as a self-loading logging truck driver weighed out, he commented to me on how fast the Snag Bay dump loader-man was. I was puzzled until he explained, "Yes, he's asleep in his loader before I even leave the dump. The only thing he does fast is get tired."

September 18

The log dump loader-man at the lake was gone at 1:00 p.m. as usual. His boss must claim full days from the Company and pay full day wages to the operator or his loader would work the full shift.

Boss said I was to travel to Snag Bay with the sort-yard loader-man but when I said, "The sort-yard loader-man arrives earlier than me and works later", I received this response, "Well then, it'll balance out."

UNWANTED DRIVING LESSONS

One loader-man could not awake to his alarm. If he awoke early, he would leave home and resume sleeping in his parked pickup in my driveway at 3:30 a.m.; noticed with great humor by the passing truckers. Sometimes he'd be on time at 5:30 a.m. and other times I took my truck to work because he was a no-show.

We traveled in an odd collection of antiquated pickups. The loader-man would not use four-wheel drive until necessary. After we spun out on the hill at the 6-kilometer sign, I'd have to get out and engage the hubs for 4-wheel drive so we could continue. At the top of the hill, the driver would stop and disengage the hubs. This procedure was repeated at incalculable inclines. We passed a loaded logging truck but the logging truck was barreling along behind us to maintain power for an adverse (uphill). I determined to myself, that if we spun out, I would run for my life up the snowbank and I would not stop to lock the hubs in.

December 21 – SNAG BAY COMMUTE

Finally, I can count on one hand the number of days left at Snag. The loader-man put a different old motor in his pickup. There is a hole in the manifold. The exhaust blowing in the cab sickens me…no lie, my eyes water…so I opened my window. Electric windows so the loader-man closes it. I open the window then put my head on the back of the seat to get air. Freezing cold air but much better than exhaust fumes. Loader-man pulls another coat from behind the seat and puts it on and then shuts the window. By then we were going downhill, and the fumes weren't as bad, and he also shut off the heater. Better cold than dead.

It was totally beautiful on our way in to Snag Bay. The sky had a touch of orange. The snow crystals were glittering like diamonds. We were in sunshine and the clouds filled the valley below us with hilltops poking through like islands. The loader-man had never seen a weather inversion before and he said, "Ha, ha, clouds below us. Wow."

Thirty kilometers from home after a winter workday at remote scales, the loader-man's pickup emitted a tremendous bang and a cloud of white smoke. No one was behind us who could assist but there may have been loggers several kilometers ahead. We had no radio communication. When the loader-man diagnosed a blown motor and my destiny may have been a night in the bush, I took off running like I had wings on my boots toward the nearest hope of help. Fortunately, loggers in the last pickup leaving the area noticed me downhill from them and I was saved! They were able to radio others to rescue the loader-man. On the next trip to work, I was surprised how many kilometers I had run uphill. Panic driven?

SNAG BAY JOURNAL

We have been putting in long days at Snag Bay. Baroff's are logging just above the scales.

Sometimes the yarder blocks the road for 1½ hours on Jim's last trip, so we have to stay really late. If Jim can't get down with his load of logs, we can't get up so what's the point of leaving on time? Mighty has been working like Superman – sometimes 9 mixed species loads into the sort-yard and 4 yard trucks hauling from the sort-yard to the lake. He said, "I'm busier than a cat trying to bury its shit on a marble floor."

HELICOPTER LOGGING

Logs dropped by a helicopter into the Snag Bay sort-yard left a tangled mess for the loader-man.

June 25 – 29 Snag Bay

Although helicopter logging was a novelty, after the first hour watching the show, it became just a noisy and dusty annoyance.

Logs were dropped in the sort-yard by the helicopter on the weekend. What a mess. Seemore, the loader-man, works late every day. He cleans up one side so the helicopter can drop logs there the next day while he is cleaning up the other side. He also has mixed loads and samples from the regular loggers arriving in the yard. I do not remember seeing him until helicopter logging ceased, yet we were on the same worksite!

July 4

Dust in the yard is brutal even at 7:00 a.m. Seemore is working in awful conditions; he can't even see his loader forks through the dust. 38 degrees today.

July 6

I hitchhike home with the last trucker most days because Seemore works so late.

Snag Bay is a dead-end road and the logging is often far, far away. It is a challenge finding a ride so I don't have to wait hours for Seemore. Some seasons, I slept in the cab of a pickup when the loader-men and loggers camped here. Bonus: I could use an electric frying pan and kettle when the generator was started in the morning. No wonder Snag Bay has so many uncomplimentary names.

SEVEN HOURS TRAVEL

One year I had to relinquish Needles for Snag Bay. The loggers threatened to cease work if the incompetent scaler was not replaced.

I hitchhiked in with loggers at 3:30 a.m. The last truck leaving the scales went to a landing to pre-load (be loaded for the morning) and got me home at 7:30 pm. No wonder the trucker and logging loader-man told me to talk to my boss about the unreasonable conditions, especially when camping in the winter was out of the question. Boss said there was nothing he could do for me. I suppose I loved my job, appreciated my co-workers and did not quit. Seagull later said Boss was paid four hours for my travel but gave me one.

A RARE VISITOR TO SNAG BAY

January 6 - Snag Bay

Frank: "The dump loader-man's boss is coming down today."
    Mighty: "Why?"
    Frank: "To see why his loader is using so much oil."
    Mighty: "It shouldn't be using much oil any more. The loader-man and his partner sold their logging truck."

SUCKERPUNCHED

MEMORABLE TRUCKS

One trucker was driving an old semi truck that lacked power. Crawling up a steep mountain pass, he was easily passed by another rig whose driver radioed, "Can't you go any faster?"

The slow trucker replied, "Yes, but it is company policy I stay with my truck."

Running two businesses is complicated and that became clear to loggers with a new ranch on that fateful day Valley Livestock Auction phoned to say the Forest Service had seized their load of logs for being branded >IH. Meanwhile, back on the Tree Farm…..

A truck is stopped at Needles scales with a legal load weight to meet road restrictions on spring highways.

NO TRUCK HEATER

Not all truckers or trucks were equal. During a bitterly cold winter at Octopus, a driver wore a snowmobile suit and gloves when his employer did not equip his truck with a heater. The windshield was continually iced up. On corners, the driver had to look out the open side window. The trucking company also skimped on chains with their solution to use an old set over a second old set, since one worn out set was like using skates. I was totally aware that at the bottom of the incredibly steep and icy haul road sat a small plywood scale shack perched like a target for runaway trucks. Competing trucking companies took pity on those drivers and offered free discarded tires to supply better rubber which was an immense improvement.

HAWK HAD A SORRY EXCUSE OF A TRUCK

November 6 – Snag Bay

Hawk's logging truck's drive shaft is only holding on by a thread. His radio doesn't work most of the time.

December 4 – Snag Bay

Hawk dumped two loads. After the second, there were noises. Aha. Hawk had hooked the air-line where the oil-line should be and the oil-line where the air-line should be. The compressor got red hot and cooked. The motor doesn't sound wonderful either. The general consensus is that he should try and get it home, out of here.

My goodness, Mighty is loading Hawk's truck but he'll probably have to tow it to the lake to dump it.

December 8 – Snag Bay

Cold day in hell. Mighty's pickup broke a radiator hose last night so he rode out with Hawk. This morning, Trucker Clen and his wife, Hawk and Mighty were in Hawk's Bronco when it broke down. They poured in all Mighty's antifreeze, water from a creek and then all their coffee before they realized there was a hole in the radiator. They were cold when we picked them up.

Air-lines were connected from one logging truck to Hawk's logging truck to enable Hawk to get his truck down the steep haul road. It was a tense time coordinating the movements of the trucks.

December 21 – Snag Bay

Hawk went to the bush…hear him coming down…wonder how long truck will last?

He hauled from the sort-yard yesterday; he can fix the truck while Mighty is loading.

Snag Bay radio is funny. This is one trip Hawk made: 'Had to get pushed up the adverse past the landing. Stuck. Lost wrapper and cinch somewhere. Went wild on a switchback. Lost chains. Logs moved ahead and have to be bucked off. Log fell off and Mighty had to put it back before he could drive onto the scales. Ten things in one trip. Today it's "Oh, I think I just went in the ditch." And "My air seems frozen."

January 3 Snag Bay

Hawk's self-loading logging truck has no brakes. This truck is not a good investment: two transmissions, rear end, hydraulic pump and motor. This 'new' (used) motor uses a lot of oil in a day.

January 4 Snag Bay

Hawk didn't have enough gas in his Bronco so rode to work with Mighty, Max and me.

Yesterday, Leroy radioed, "What is that yard truck doing parked on the road off the scales?"

I said, "No brakes."

Lee said, "What if I can't stop?"

"Oh," I said, "Don't run into Hawk's truck or he'll have to spend $300 for a new one."

Hawk's truck was getting antifreeze into the engine at Snag Bay. He had checked the oil dipstick and there was antifreeze on it. To get his rig home, he drained the radiator and filled it with diesel. Well, that solved the problem of antifreeze getting into the oil.

NEEDLES SCALES

Hawk clanked onto the scales and his logging truck died. The batteries were no good so it would not start. He had to get towed off with a loader. There was a lidless kettle hanging from the underside of the truck. This was an efficient way to collect leaking oil since the spout made it easy to pour back into the motor. Twice Hawk announced on his arrival he'd taken out power lines.

A joke circulated about Hawk being stopped by the police. The truck, it transpired, had slick tires, no horn, no lights, no windshield wipers, had air leaks and oil leaks. Also, it was overloaded and had no brakes. The cop said, "I think the best way to charge you is 'hauling wood without a truck."

TRUCKERS BEGAN WORK VERY EARLY IN THE MORNING

One chilly morning at Needles, Jo was late bringing his load to the scales. In fact, he was <u>very</u> late, although we had seen his loaded truck across the road at the shop when we drove to work. We assumed he had mechanical problems until he admitted he had started his cold logging truck and crawled back into his warm pickup where he enjoyed a long unintentional sleep.

GREEN DRIVER

Dan told us when he was a green trucker, he hauled a load over the Monashee pass. When he got to the brake check at the top of Mine Hill, it was plugged with trucks so he carried on without stopping. He white-knuckled it down the hill to the amazement of all the experienced drivers parked at the top. Dan discovered later all the other rigs were parked waiting for a sand truck.

BAD LUCK DAY

January 2 Needles

Bob, Ivan, Neil and Wally's trucks are broken down. Dennis drove off the cattle guard (*grating used to catch mud before the scales*) and Brad flopped his truck.

Trey hit his steering box on the sample skids. I called Forest Service for permission to estimate the truck's empty weight if he can't drive back onto the scales. I can, but I must cancel and replace the sample if it's not an actual weight.

A view of the Needles log dump attracts onlookers to the Arrow Lakes ferry railing.

The season a Grand Forks contractor planned to replace wheel loaders at sort-yards with a Butt'n'top track loader was a doomed, dismal failure. The cartoon depicts the horrible conditions spending that season at Snag Bay.

A self-loading truck stopped on the new Needles scales with a load of cedar.

A load of spruce is weighed on the Needles scales.

Logging trucks are used in adverse conditions, on poor roads and some in poor mechanical condition.

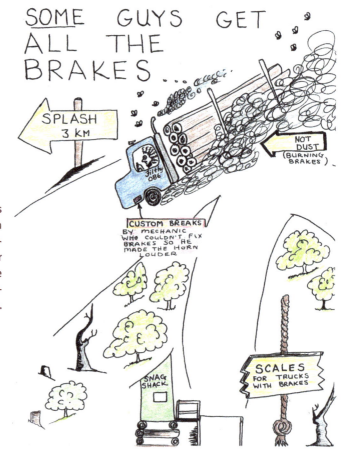

Roads under construction were soft and caused this truck to tip over.

Yard trucks were often not up to acceptable standards since they only hauled from the sort-yard to the log dump at the lake. Snag Bay scales, however, was 3 kilometers from the lake. A truck pulled from a junkyard could recover more than its value in a week but pity the driver who futilely asked for rudimentary repairs.

NAKUSP TRUCKER – a poem by L. Wood

Met a guy in Wylie's who owned a truck
And had a million after only a year.
Dollars, that is, in the bank. Cash.
Bought that truck and bought him a beer.

Alarm went off before wife's gone to bed,
Packed my lunch, kissed my honey.
Off to the landing, wood's waiting to haul,
Got me a truck, going to make money.

Sold my car and fishing boat to Petrocan,
Mortgaged the house and got insurance.
Kal Tire accepted my Mastercard,
But this is a million- dollar chance.

Pope's cut the rates, so I spend four
And know I'll get paid for two,
Hours, that is. Money lost. Gone.
Have me a truck, no time to be blue.

The first month seemed kinda slow
And the million was hard to see;
A rear end gone, steering tire too,
Trying to make it up and D.O.T. got me.

The weekends are for truck repair,
Oil changes and a pressure wash.
I don't miss the boat I used to have,
I've got no time to fish, by gosh.

Saw strangers in my house,
Got my gun, called nine-one-one.
They said, "Don't shoot us, you fool.
We're only your wife and son!"

SUCKERPUNCHED

Met the guy who sold me the truck
And had a million after only a year,
Dollars, that is. In the bank. Cash.
My ($#@*&^$) million sure isn't here.

I said, "Buy me a beer. I'm broke.
I was had, you liar, you cheat.
No house left, no car, nothing at all.
I gave it a year, but I am beat."

That guy had tears in his eyes,
Said, "Lying and cheating I never do.
I had a million after a year,
But didn't you hear I'd started with two?"

Two self-loading trucks are at the Snag Bay scales.

In the 1980s, a truck drove out of control from a haul road, through a shop yard and over a bank. The truck stakes are silhouetted on the skyline. The cab and exhaust stack are visible under the logs. The driver survived with minor injuries.

In 2007, a car speeding down the highway ran under a logging truck crossing the highway to Needles scales. A trucker radioed the scales and said, "I just ran over a car." I asked, "Should I call an ambulance?" The driver replied, "I don't know. I haven't gotten out of my truck yet to see." The horror in his voice was obvious. Amazingly, the two males in the car escaped nearly injury-free. Although the passengers escaped their car on their own, and were walking with no apparent serious injuries, I suggested they go by ambulance for medical attention. The scales remained open even as I worked around stretchers, paramedics, patients and blood.

An Okanagan logging truck left a log yard near the Needles scales with a load. The driver decided to travel on a logging road paralleling the highway before reconnecting with the highway. He had no chains and no radio communication with the local traffic. He promptly spun out on the snowy hill, slid backwards and spilled logs over the highway. I immediately called the ferry to warn traffic of the road closure and prevent a further disaster. A loader from the Needles scales cleared the blockage, although the load had not originated there.

This truck went straight, although the highway curved, en route to Needles.

A truck from Kamloops crashed on Highway 6
a short distance from the Needles scales.
Nobody was injured. The driver had failed to adequately slow for the corner.

LOG SCALERS

Logs can have rot. Rot and other defects may severely impact lumber recovery at the sawmill. Do scalers have x-ray vision? No, but an excellent sense of assessing the logs can be developed to correctly scale for volume and quality of merchantable wood.

IGNORANT ERRORS AND DISGRACEFUL DISREGARD FOR SCALING

Avoidable errors were caused when a scaler did not inspect the loads of logs.

A loader-man radioed, "The sample load of balsam (alpine fir) is spread for you to scale".

I looked on the list of samples to scale and did not find a balsam load, only lodgepole. I checked the weigh slip. Even the load advice slip from the logging site said, 'Species: Lodgepole.' The scaler had recorded a balsam load as lodgepole; she did not leave her desk to inspect loads.

When Boss notified the scaler, she showed no comprehension of scaling responsibilities and no desire to learn. If only one load out of seventy was randomly selected by the computer as a sample, how many more were wrong?

October 22

We had no breaks at all today. The loader-man, Rob, wants a second scaler so we can catch up on all the samples that need to be scaled. If I don't get help, does that make me helpless?

He said a scaler didn't want to make out 2 tickets for a load that was half cedar pulp and half larch sawlogs and when it came up a sample, he had the loader-man replace cedar with larch.

October 23 Needles

I phoned Boss to ask if anyone was coming to help scale samples and he said, "No."

I'd asked for someone to help scale samples and fill in the last ½ hour so I could make it to my doctor's appointment. Boss said, "Doctors are always late anyways."

Mine is usually on time. I phoned the Nakusp clinic and cancelled my appointment.

A loader-man said a 100% spruce load was entered in the computer as balsam and it came up a sample. The loader-man told the scaler to put it in the lake, replace it with the next load of balsam and not say anything. The weight of the second load was 53,000kg and the ticket for the first load said 67,000kg. The conversion was 0.7. (Balsam should be 1.2.)

One scaler was unpopular. When a load of sawlogs had one discoloured log end, he recorded the entire load as pulp. There were no bad logs sent to the sawmill and there were wonderful loads of sawlogs chipped for pulp.

The loggers threatened to stop work if the problems were not dealt with.

THE BAD

Scaler error caused a small logging company a large monetary loss. The Company paid the logger according to the inaccurate scale; his anticipated profits vanished. His salvaged dry fir was put in a 'green' category with the scaler saying there was no other choice.

If a load of logs did not fit the strata criteria, it was to be 'Red Tagged' and hand scaled to determine the actual volume, grades and species. Following the rules created necessary work to a scaler and should never have been avoided.

THE UGLY

An employer brazenly and openly changed log data. A Forest Service check scaler, experienced, but never challenged, his behavior. Her comment to me, that he was likely acting on behalf of a timber company employee who bragged at how many millions of dollars he saved the company, hit me like a hammer. At what cost, and to whom?

Apparently, this dishonest scaler had no remorse for his actions and frequently divulged incidents. It was like being gut-punched to hear him say his computer crashed and lost scale data on eleven loads at three mill-sites on a Saturday. Did he return on Sunday to re-do the loads? No, he fabricated all of them.

DISHONESTY COULD REAP REWARDS TO A FEW; LOSSES TO OTHERS

If ten hand scaled samples apply a factor to six hundred loads, but the conversion is deliberately lowered, a logger may lose $300 a load and the government would lose stumpage payable. The timber company gains those costs and also saws more lumber.

In three months, on low value logs, a pulp company lost over $100,000 attributed to scaler errors in stratification. A stratum for 100% hemlock had the first sample loads scaled with a combined hemlock content of 59%. The previous year, the conversion was 0.99 but the scaler errors caused an over conversion of 1.47. (The weight of the load is multiplied by the stratum conversion to calculate the volume.)

Forest Service check scales were supposed to be random and unannounced. The last load I hand scaled had to be available for examination.

When a check scaler kept my employer informed of where and when the checks would be made, he was able to scale the load for incapable scalers in their name. Between times, the inferior scaling continued.

As I helped a scaler with six years employment with Boss, he asked me to tell him when we got to a spruce. The first 38 logs had been spruce; he'd entered them as balsam. His grading and rot calculations were equally as bad. If check scale loads had not been scaled by someone else using his name, he'd likely have lost his license.

Manly, a co-worker, and I shared laughter, but more importantly, the desire to scale at the highest level we could. With proof, Manly reported dishonest scaling and soon after lost his job.

With so many variables between loads of logs and individual logs, I was always a student with learning required until retirement. I maintained a diligent effort to achieve scaling accuracy. My journals recorded my Forest Service check scale results and my accuracy in challenging determinations for stratifying loads: percentages of species, grades and quality in every load of logs.

Was I an extra-ordinary Superwoman? No. I was fulfilling my obligations as a licensed log scaler.

PICK YOUR RUT CAREFULLY – YOU'LL BE IN IT FOR THE NEXT 80 KM

We tried to get to Snag Bay one early morning. A skidder, trying to open the road ahead of us, ran out of fuel. Our pickup had mechanical problems and stopped all traffic behind us. Trees, overburdened with heavy wet snow, were bent over the roadway compounding our difficulties.

ROUGH ROADS

The rocky road to Snag Bay could be unbearably rough.

One morning, we were surprised to see a 'Grader Working' sign as we began our usual arduous trip to Snag Bay. This was pleasant news. Graders were harder to find along that bouncy road than Santa Claus or the Easter

Bunny. After many kilometers, we realized the joke – that the truckers had stolen the sign. This garnered many a chuckle before the sign was returned to its rightful owner.

Accessing scales could be a challenge during the winter. Unplowed roads were commonplace, inspiring the following cartoon's caption:

Newsflash! The timber company will save $7,822,100 by cutting snow removal costs. The shortage of graders leads to cost costing strategies. A slight delay in opening roads after snowfalls can be tolerated. The company has effectively eliminated the dependence on unreliable mechanical devices.

A load of large spruce logs arriving at Snag Bay scales.

SUCKERPUNCHED

September 9 – Snag Bay

If Bore, the company accountant, ever calls to tell me to send data, I should say, "I'll send data when you'all send us a grader." The road was graded when we started here a month and a half ago. The road is extremely rough: washed from downpours, logging over it in a few places and yarder, processor, loader on the road in three cut blocks. We bounce 88 km. a day in the truck. Today we had four in the cab because no one picked Don up.

Snag Bay needs a full-time chiropractor.

INTERESTING RIDES TO WORK

December 20 – Snag Bay

The loader-man's truck is sick. It's a different one again. The automatic transmission does not work; if it had to shift it would stay in neutral. The motor sounds like a can of rocks. Even as the cab is filling with thick acrid smoke, he says nothing.

July 17 – Snag Bay

Sunny day in Snag. Truck died on way in…backfired and burned and we had to tape wires and push-start the truck.

November 9 – Snag Bay

Was it E.S.P. that I called Mighty for a ride to work? The other loader-man was late. He said only one wheel on his truck works and 4- wheel drive doesn't work at all so he had to get towed up the 21 km. hill and that's why he was late. I never asked him to explain how only one wheel can work.

I DON'T MIND GOING TO WORK, IT'S THE LONG WAIT TO GO HOME THAT BOTHERS ME.

Sometimes the longest wait wasn't time spent at the scales, but the travel, especially for remote scales.

Generally, the policy was the scaler traveled to the scales with a loader-man. Too frequently, this system failed me. At times, I drove the loader operator to work in my truck. I slept in the cab of a pickup when no rides were available to get me home. I hitchhiked to and from work with loggers spending seven hours a day traveling.

Hours from pavement and home, the loader-man's pickup slid down an icy road into the ditch and crashed into rocks. Fortunately, we were not injured, had a radio and could call for assistance. Prior experiences without a radio, and the loggers leaving the area ahead of us, meant help could be forthcoming only after we were no-shows back in civilization.

Maintaining skills at a training day. Note rotten centres in cedar. Scaler: Steve Wood

QUALITY CONTROL

The scalers were responsible for reporting the quality of the logs to the office staff and the loggers responsible. Official forms are used for recording load infractions or a note can be entered on the computer and downloaded nightly to the office. A weigh slip allows for remarks such as: 'Needles needs felt pens and printer ribbons', 'This load has 7 top diameters under 4 inches', or 'This load has 4 rotten butts.'

PAPER TOWELS

Manly made a note on his computer: 'Paper towels.' The entire office was baffled over the meaning of the note so two employees drove to his scales, one hour away, to ask for an explanation. They queried, "Does 'paper towels' mean there were pulp logs in the load?"

The scaler replied, "No, it means I need paper towels." His boss, always pennywise, advised the scaler to go to town, buy a roll of paper towels but save the receipt so the company could reimburse Boss.

URGENT REQUEST FOR WEIGH SLIPS

One scaler may have wished he'd made a note on his computer data transfer long before he radioed the office with an urgent message saying he had no weigh slips left. The supervisor questioned the demand but the scaler reiterated there were no weigh slips. The supervisor raced to the scale site, an hour away, with the necessary forms but as he entered the scale shack, he noticed the scaler in a chair with his feet resting on a box. His footrest was full of weigh slips. Oops.

AM I CRAZY?

During an extremely hectic spell at Needles, I wrote a computer note, 'If you think you can drive me crazy, you are too late.'

My supervisor yelled over the phone, "WHAT IS THAT SUPPOSED TO MEAN?"

I meekly and apologetically explained, "I only meant it as a joke."

EXTRA-ORDINARY LOAD INSPECTION

1991 Needles

Nels did safety inspections and quality checks on my quality checks. Once, he questioned my call of bush run (mix of big and small logs) on a Lumby truck.

He explained the contractors were told the maximum diameter for small log loads was 16 inches but actually 18 inches was okay, and the mill would accept 20 inches. Nels eyed a log on the top of the load and scampered up to the top of the load to measure it. While he was standing on the truck's tri-axle reach, he said, "This is why you should wear caulk boots."

Lawrence, the driver, replied sarcastically, "Steel on steel? I don't think so."

Bob, impatiently waiting in his truck behind Lawrence, said he'd have driven to the lake with Nels atop his load. Nels' final verdict? The log was 22 inches in diameter so my call of bush run was acceptable.

TOO MUCH BLAME

One scaler received a disciplinary notice, with employment termination threatened, after the sawmill didn't get their projected lumber recovery after sawing fir. The scaler was blamed because a portion of the fir sawn was sweepy and said to have originated from his scales. The scaler maintained futilely that quality issues with his logs had been reported from the scales but the poor logs had been purchased from the East Kootenay. *(Sweepy trees are not straight, usually from growing on rocky slopes.)*

Another scaler was blamed for accepting checked pine that affected lumber recovery. In fact, the logs had been left in the mill yard over a hot dry summer and certainly developed checks over that time. *(Checks are cracks that develop as a log dries.)*

Note from a co-worker: 'Rig, a loader-man, said he went to a company meeting. A scaler, not us, put sawlog tags on a pulp load and the bundled load came up onto the sawmill deck and was opened up during a sawmill tour. What a blatant scaler blunder to have rotten hemlock in the sawmill! The company guys at the meeting said it was the dump loader operator's fault because he dumped it in the lake. True story, if you believe Rig.'

Journal entry

I am in trouble if I report too many log quality infractions because it looks like there's too much wrong and Seagull isn't doing his job. I'm in trouble if I report too little because then the scaler is blamed for not doing their job by looking at the logs in the load.

Appears that shit falls downhill.

When a logging contractor reported another contractor's trucks for hauling unsafe loads, the drivers arrived at the scales furious. They did not discount the danger their loader-man presented by putting short logs on the load because those can be easily dislodged; rather it was the manner of the reporting contractor. 'Shorts on a load' is a company quality infraction but to ease the tension, I temporarily stapled various kinds of cloth shorts, like Bermuda shorts, to a load of logs with a sign and arrow stating 'Shorts in Load' and posted the photograph on the wall. When Boss noticed the picture, he glared at it and gruffly demanded, "Whose truck is that?" I may have read too many Mad Magazines as a kid and Boss certainly did not appreciate my warped sense of humor that ensued.

SUPERVISORS AND BOSSES

Seagull was our company supervisor who delighted in being loud and intimidating. Having the scaling contractor, our boss, literally cower in his presence was his forte but the scalers' misfortune since fear kept our boss from confronting injustices.

When we had computer problems, Seagull reacted quickly. It was the inconsistencies that were the most challenging for us. A scaler could be told he did a good job while others heard he was the absolute worst.

July 4 - Snag Bay

Seagull gave me a suspender type of hi-visibility reflective gear and said next time he saw me he wanted me wearing that…and only that.

How rude.

BOSSES

My various bosses had scaling contracts with the timber company.

One day, Rick, a Forest Service check scaler, brought three scaling office clerks for a tour. I had seen a guy walking over the decks in the sort yard and figured him to be a Westar (Company) quality man or forester. He came in the scale shack and recognized Rick. The clerks were suggesting tying Forest Service copies of weigh slips together with elastic bands or string. I replied, "Oh this cheap outfit! I don't have any supplies like that."

The clerks and Rick left, then the mystery guy said, "Hi, I'm Tim."

I asked, "What do you do? Forester? Log buyer?"

Tim said, "I sign your checks." Oops. This was the first time I had met my boss. I felt the only time I didn't have my foot in my mouth was when I was changing feet.

He laughed; I kept my job, especially when I proved my capabilities as a scaler.

He told me I couldn't get help to scale samples unless I was more than 5 behind. I'd have 5 to do, scale 2, receive 2 more sample loads, and so on for months. Loads were hand scaled a few lengths and diameters at a time with continual interruptions to weigh trucks. The scales were busy, usually 70 loads from the bush and 20 from the sort yard.

The Forest Service conducted full audits at the scales; they checked all the entries on all the (pre-computer) paperwork. They conducted a check scale and found no errors.

One boss was intimidated by Seagull. Scalers knew Boss never deviated from Seagull's opinion because, as we were told, "I have to side with him because he signs my cheques."

PUNISHMENT FOR A FUNERAL

I phoned my boss seconds after I received a devastating phone call, but he did not hear me say, "It's a family crisis and I don't want to talk about it right now."

I was severely hurt by a long verbal outburst, "What am I supposed to do? Where is the computer going to be? I need more warning than this…."

My father had unexpectedly passed away from a mountain biking accident, a few weeks after my mother's sudden death.

This is the transcript of a phone call from Boss before I returned to Snag Bay from the compassionate leave:

> Boss: 'Um, uh a loader-man has your computer. Um uh uh, it's a different one. There's a um uh power cord um huh uh to um modem out.'
>
> Lois: 'I plug the modem into the power cord?'

Boss: 'Um uh what do you call the thing the printers plug into?'

Lois: 'I have no idea what you are talking about.'

Boss: 'Um uh you'll see it um.'

Lois: 'What kind of computer do I have?'

Boss: 'I think um uh ah uh Toshiba.'

Lois: 'That's what I had.'

Boss: ' Um uh well it's um uh might um huh, you'll see it.'

WHEN I RETURNED TO WORK, I FACED A HUGE BACKLOG OF WORK.

I cannot figure out the computer. I cannot get the weighmaster to respond and had to enter weights into the computer manually. Then I see no samples are scaled. The replacement scaler was told by Boss not to bother scaling any while I was at my Dad's funeral.

Even Seagull supported the Boss because I had woken Boss at 9:45 p.m. when I heard my dad had passed and asked for time off work. I suspected I was accused of deliberately antagonizing the Boss for a solely ulterior motive and their feelings never vaporized with the truth, they intensified.

Seagull unfairly chastised scalers who even endured rude phone calls at home. One response to an innocuous question about measuring logging waste was, "You are so stupid, if I had a gun I would shoot you,"

Aware they had no support from their employer, despite his knowledge of complaints, the employees learned to cope on their own.

COMMUNICATION DIFFICULTIES

June 14

I left a message on Boss' answering machine: 'I need 18th and 19th off' after my friend said, "It's <u>surgery</u>, take an extra day off!" I then spent a long time awake in bed afraid of his reaction for taking two days instead of only one.

November 27

I have a bad cold, so I told Boss I needed tomorrow off.

November 28

I went to the Outpost hospital and the diagnosis is worse than a cold. No wonder I feel so sick.

When I asked for another day off (Friday), Boss flipped; He needed me to work because he'll be working at Fosthall. I relinquished but I need to get well!

October 22 - Needles

Monday, I started telling Boss that I had lots of problems. (Fortunately, none of them itch.) Maybe because of power surges causing battery backup to keep kicking in, the printers screwed up and because the printers went off, the computer screwed up. He just walked out without a comment.

It's dark in the a.m., dark in the p.m. and I'm in the dark all day with Windows 95.

November 15 - Needles

I gave Boss the stapler used to fasten load tags. He had tools out working on his loader. I explained the stapler was jammed and asked if he could please fix it. He immediately handed it back to me and told me to keep it for a spare.

I was puzzled and said, "But it's broken".

A loader-man watching suggested to Boss, "Give your head a shake."

Boss then handed me a broom. Now I was really puzzled but when I questioned it, he explained, "Maybe you will want to sweep the scale deck sometime."

I managed the repair myself.

Seagull said he looks at Boss's eyes and when they are vacant, his head is spinning and there is no use trying to talk to him.

OKAY TO GO HOME.... BUT LEAVE THE PICKUP

The sort-yard loader operator, Mighty, went home for personal reasons when the yard truck never showed up at Snag Bay and we did not need two loader-men. He offered to return for us at the end of the day. To save him two hours' travel, we arranged a ride with a logging crew.

When Boss heard we had not traveled home with Mighty, he complained to Mighty's employer. When I asked him, "Why?" he explained, "Mighty's employer is responsible for driving you to and from work."

He emphatically defended reporting Mighty's actions, "He should have left you the pickup."

When an incident arose that required levelheaded compromising or understanding, one boss metamorphosed from a meek mouse to a raging animal, unbelievable to those who never witnessed the transformation.

A scaler attempted to discuss work entitlements and harassment with Boss only to announce in frustration, she would never try to approach him again.

We all learned to just 'suck it up'.

Many expressed shock that I continued to work under such an employer but I enjoyed my job. I definitely was given many opportunities to fail. I was told Boss was personally bothered by how I excelled at my job. Conversely, poor scaling was disguised rather than attempting to improve standards.

Scalers were told by Boss, "Lying is just good business."

COMPUTERS ARE NOT INTELLIGENT. THEY ONLY THINK THEY ARE.

Pity Albert, our computer programmer and personal instructor. He was responsible for computer upgrades; he took old bugs out and put new ones in.

Most of us thought 'log on' was what we did to get the wood stove hotter, 'download' was getting the firewood off the truck, 'modem' was what we did to the hayfields and 'hard drive' was getting home in the wintertime.

With Albert's patient coaching, we soon learned a lot about computers. We found out that computers make very fast, very accurate mistakes. Our policy was to always blame the computer. Didn't it say, 'Press any key to continue or any other key to quit?'

When printer or computer problems arose, they were usually accompanied by profanity and quick attempts to rectify the quandary since the truckers did not want to be delayed.

Darwin, the office accountant, and Albert were unbelievably tolerant and could calmly talk me through every step necessary to rectify a problem.

One scaler's performance when a malfunction occurred was amusing, in fact it put me into near hysterics. He jumped around, pounded the offending electronic contraption, spoke to it in less than endearing terms and even threw his hard hat on the floor.

Not all our problems were operator caused. My scales were set up with faulty equipment, known not to work at previous locations. When I radioed to report the malfunctions, I was told my faulty computer had screwed up only twice in the time Red used it, therefore it would repeat that pattern of monthly breakdowns for me. Seagull yelled, "What did you do to it? It didn't quit that often before!"

SNAG BAY – COMPUTER NOTEPAD TO ACCOUNTANT

For many of us, the first experience with computers occurred in the workplace. This was certainly true with scaling. One day, we scalers discovered that old slow data terminals had been replaced by sleek efficient computers with keys that said scary things like 'num lock' and 'crtl'. Fortunately, we were trained by highly skilled professional personnel. We were wary at first, but after just 175 weeks of training, we discovered that, instead of delivering old-fashioned paper, we could create lengthy articles on screen and then, by simply pushing a button, send them to …the planet Zomber. "What the h--- is wrong with our PC!!!" we would shout but the errors always turned out to be our fault. But gradually we got the hang of it, and today we routinely use highly sophisticated multi-million-dollar systems to perform a function vital to scaling….

Namely sending personal messages to one another.

Snag Bay – computer notepad to accountant

Well, Snag Scales enters the computer age with a mouse for the computer. I don't know why people think a mouse is such a big deal; it keeps leaving turds in my printer. Want a rat for your computer? I can supply those too but bigger is not better.

January 20 – computer notepad from accountant, Bob, to all scalers

Yes, sports fans, I am alive! Rumors of my demise are greatly exaggerated. Now would someone please stop my wife, as she is trying to cash in on my life insurance!

January 21 – computer notepad to accountant, Bob, from Lois

So, you are not dead. That is happy news. We wondered why being a bean counter was deadly.

Accountant: a job to die for? Where accountants go to die? Dead people can't count. Are you really going to die there? Is that covered by compo? What does the company do with the bodies? I thought the last accountant left rather abruptly.

From all the intelligence emitted from your office, we had assumed you were already dead.

October 18 – computer notepad from accountant, Bob, to Lois

Happy birthday. The oldest woman to ever walk into Bear Lake. They say that wine gets better as it gets older. Too bad the same isn't true about women. Just think of all the things to look forward to: grandchildren, menopause, pension, Geritol, Reno. Menopause is actually spelled "men no!! pause?"

August 17 – Snag Bay – computer notepad to accountant

Snowballs in hell. A trucker threw a snowball at me from white stuff on his hood. White country from 8 km. on Johnston road (5 km. above scales) to past water tower on way home. Arrgghh! (*The 'water tower' was the site where trucks filled up with water for old-time brakes.*)

Isn't this supposed to be summer?

August 23 – Snag Bay computer notepad to accountant

Today the loader-man asked, in all seriousness, "Thunder is from two clouds banging together, but what causes lightning?"

September 29 – Snag Bay – computer notepad to accountant

Some paperwork got as far as Needles. Sending 28th and 29th data.

Last truck last night never weighed out until today. It's not because we're slow or time stands still at Snag. I arrived home at 8 p.m. previous night. Ride in the next a.m. was at 4:00. Radiator hose broke on logging truck so he could not dump. Could get ride out at 5:00 p.m. and didn't want to pass that up.

Saw other life forms today on trip out to sort-of-civilization…tourist fishermen types from Grand Forks with two flat tires.

January 21 – computer notepad from Bob (accountant)

Dear Snag. I used to think that the woman scaler we had working at Needles had a sense of humor. Lately though, it seems she has a big case of writer's cramp.

Is there any way we can spur her creativity once more, so as to brighten our coffee breaks?

January 22 – computer notepad to Bob (accountant)

You miss my insults? My degrading putdowns? Well…you'll get notes now we're getting fewer loads.

Poor little overworked Snag

February 8 – Needles scales - Computer notepad to accountant

Okay, who was that on the radio who asked if I was glad to be back in civilization from Snag Bay? And if I had shaved off my beard and put on nice clothes?

JOURNAL ENTRIES

Needles has issues. One printer is totally screwed. The other one has alarm light on, all 'print qualities', 'char pitch' lights on plus 'menu' and 'quiet.' It did print the last ticket okay. I get Seagull tomorrow and as he goes crazy, I will go outside and scale samples. All the machines are back from repair service. There is all new wiring from computer to printers and a new data switch box. All the problems prior to breakup are still happening!

I lost some loads in the Snag Bay computer. Aliens? No, it was because the scales were set with too small of parameters and moving inside the shack would cause enough motion to cause failure. The computer prompted, "Motion. Retry y/n." before the scale technician was able to diagnose and fix it.

Octopus scales was a change from hectic Stobo scales; Lars was the only trucker, so we had 4 loads a day. One day, the scale weight continually changed, rising by increments to 80,000 kg and dropping 20 kg at a time to -80,000 kg then rising, and then dropping. When Seagull arrived to fix it, he discovered a bare scale wire (chewed by rats) and moisture had caused the problem.

SELF-LOADING TRUCK
NEEDLES

BETWEEN AND AFTER WORK

Whoever doesn't believe that the dead can come to life, should be here at quitting time.

COW CHORES

Wintertime was a mad scramble for me after work. Sometimes there was quickly disappearing daylight when the cows and horses could be fed and actually seen. Usually, with only the faint light of a flashlight, I pulled hay bales into a melee of hungry black cows with a toboggan. Hay was spread out in another pasture, so the morning's chore simply entailed opening a gate. Supper was started and when my spouse returned from his job, he could shovel and plow snow.

Summertime meant a different set of chores: haying and gardening mostly. Fire season engaged my spouse, and usually meant I coped without help.

One morning, I hurried to lock a huge nasty cow in the barn, dodging her massive horns. The objective was for her to adopt a calf, but she was not at all thrilled about that.

I'd cut nice green grass and clover to entice her to put her head in the stanchion although it was apparent it had a laxative effect and created semi-liquid, slippery manure. Keeping an eye on my watch and trying to be speedy and efficient, I guided the calf to the cow's udder. When I tried to pull the calf away to put her in her pen, it seems the calf had been gaining weight and strength because I had lost the advantage I once had. My feet had no traction on the loosey-goosey poo and down I went. I didn't feel that I lingered on the barn floor any more than I would hold my hand on a hot stove. I thought I barely touched for a milli-second, but

I was soaked through coveralls and jeans to my skin. A quick bath and change of clothes and I was off to work, in a hurry and feeling like I should have soaked in the bath longer. Terry and the other truckers definitely agreed and chuckled over my latest anecdote.

WAITING FOR A RIDE TO WORK

The computer, in its large suitcase-looking case, had to be taken home at night to download the day's data to the office. While my truck spent time with a mechanic, the loader-man refused money to backtrack a few kilometers to pick me up. The sole alternative was to pull my computer and lunch box to the highway on a toboggan to catch a seven- minute ride with loggers. I sat in a snowbank for an hour until the loader-man picked me up. If the town-folk had seen me, I am sure interesting gossip circulated: picture a sorry, cold woman with two suitcases at 4:30 a.m. looking for a ride out of town up a dead- end snowy logging road.

MANLY VS. LOIS

Manly replied to my scaling jokes and it evolved into an exchange of letters and jokes delivered by truckers and check scalers. Rereading them now, I am struck by how much fun we had. We also shared serious scaling matters. (The following is from various years in no particular order.)

December 6 – letter from Manly to Lois

Sometime, I'd like to talk to you in person *(We actually went a year without meeting.)* There is so much about this job that you just have to talk to another scaler. Really helps me. If the loaders spread a load in the afternoon, and it gets snowed on, it's easy to miss a grade 4 because of rotten knots or twist. I'm not worried about being caught by the check scalers, I just don't want to miss anything. If it's a grade 4, I want every chance to find it, whereas before grading, it was pretty much only a volume scale so not such a big deal.

Fortunately, Rig is really good at giving me a portion of a load at a time or not spreading until the weather changes. If we don't stratify to a high degree of excellence, we should not be in the position of scaler.

Somehow, a friendly competition evolved between Manly and me as to who was Number One.

September 30 – letter from Manly to Lois:

Of course, I believed everything you said. There has never been any BS in any of your letters except the time you thought you won.

October 27 – letter to Manly:

(Manly had gone socializing with the check scalers after work.)

You always get a good check scale because you go drinking with the check scalers so take them out tonight and buy them a drink from me and I'll get a good check scale.

October 31 – letter from Manly –delivered with glee by the check scalers

I will enclose a receipt *(an official looking Visa receipt for $411.34)*. I sure do appreciate you wanting to buy the check scalers a drink. You should come up sometime.

Krill came down once. But we told her how stupid truckers are. Naturally, with her dad, uncles and boyfriend being in the business, she tried to stick up for them, much to our amusement and not hers.

November 6 – Needles – letter to Manly from Lois

(Long before this, we made aluminum tags for the loads with an embosser, made for printing credit cards in a previous life.)

Thank you for giving me a copy of your credit card receipt. I still have an embosser at Needles and was able to perfect a duplicate card. And I've practiced your signature.

I am enclosing personalized pencils: 'Lois' scales - P&T's best'.

(I visited the Lodge bar after this and was informed by the manager that I had a $400 tab there and he'd like it cleared up. Manly and I were not the only ones who enjoyed the jesting.)

September 25- Snag Bay- letter to Manly

The check scalers were here. My volume was 38.81; their volume was 38.81 on a rather ugly fir load. They had a grade difference, a rot, and I ended up with 0.5% difference for value. I don't even have to go socializing with them.

November 25 – letter from Manly at Fosthall scales

This is great. I haven't had a sample for TWO DAYS. Looking out the window watching it snow. When the truckers come in, I sing, "Walking in a winter wonderland and let it snow, let it snow…"

Packed rock to both sides of the scales to fill in mud holes, about 300 gallons as I pack it in 5-gallon buckets. Shoveled wet gooey mud off the scales, vacuumed, washed the floor, washed the windows. Computer is about to ring sample in just about every stratum.

Snag Bay – letter to Manly

We have two yard trucks today. One of them drives to the lake and the other tries to guess which one it was.

September 14 - letter from Manly at Fosthall scales

Well, I just stuck my nose where it doesn't belong again. We have three loaders in the sort-yard and one dumping at the lake. We get here in the morning and the dump machine won't start so don't just take a yard loader to the beach, no, two loaders try to get one loader going and the trucks are waiting at the beach.

So, I walked out and said, "Why don't you dump the trucks and then get this one started?" so I'll be the donkey butt again today. Need curtains, have to shut my radio off, need blinders, earplugs, tongue cut out, bag over my head and slapped.

July 4 – Needles – letter to Manly

Boss fixed the handheld scaling computer Nik broke which is why Nik got mine. Guess what was wrong? Nik forgot about the lighten and darken screen key, he kept hitting the key and the screen went black.

February 23 – letter from Manly at Fosthall

I think it would be nice to have contact with other scalers, but it is an untrusting world.

Yesterday was trouble city. Chris went over the bank and had to unload (*Self loading 'hook' truck*) then get the grader to pull him out. Richard hit the ditch and did in one bumper, one fender, headlights and blinker lights. Doug (*a logging contractor*) was driving his own logging truck. He told his skidder operator to "COME HERE". The skidder man drove over, but the skidder didn't stop and smashed into the logging truck. Oops, one fender.

Snag Bay – to co-worker

I haven't seen the sort-yard loader-man for <u>weeks</u>, a lot of weeks. He never stops even for coffee. He just about got all the mixed loads sorted and decked, then skidders and bush loaders broke down and the trucks came to haul from the sort-yard to the lake.

February 7 – Needles – letter to Manly

(Truckers delivered notes from one scale site to another.)

Bob brought your letter in, but it sure bugged him. I told him the truth that usually you send me garbage and scrap paper, so I am sure he feels like a really important mailman.

October 25 – letter from Manly

Cheez. Remember I told you I shoveled the scale deck off nice and clean? Well, Bill just came in. He stops on the scales; he's 80 seconds ahead of his cycle time so he starts knocking the mud off his truck. Scalers should be allowed to pack guns: Boom, yah *****, need another driver.

January 17 – letter from Manly

The other day I was proud of myself. I had all the ice and snow off my scales, took the middle rubber off and was getting rid of the ice under the mats. Neil drives on, looks at my scales and says, "You should see Lois' scales, it's spotless."

What the **** is going on, Suzy Homemaker? Are you trying to make me look bad? Next time I'm there, if Neil's around, I'm going to shovel snow on your scales.

December 8 - Needles - to Manly

A trucker said Nik has blown up 3 hand-held scaling computers and 4 weigh ticket computers because he pounds the keys. Hask said he timed a weigh in at Halfway scales and it was 11 minutes.

Quit spoiling the truckers, 11 minutes is quite reasonable. You do not have to put a truck through in 3 minutes. Did you train Hask? I went to get a ticket from the printer, and he said, "Are you that slow putting supper on the table? Manly would have had me weighed in by now."

February 16 - letter from Manly

Only 11 loads so far today. I like being a wait scaler. Watch and wait - what a lifestyle. Work, I just wait. Supper, I just wait. Even fishing, throw the lines out and wait. Only problem is too much weight.

February 2 - letter from Manly

(One loader-man's name is Les so the second loader-man was called 'More'.)

'Just went out to help More tighten his chains. Bill is back operating a loader. He broke his leg last Friday but, being the man that he is, it's healed already. When he came in the scale shack to tell me about it, I told him, "No, it's not broken."

He said, "Maybe it's cracked."

I said, "It's not cracked, either."

Today, Monday, all the way to work he's telling us how sore it is. Then he says the doctor sent the x-rays away. I felt like saying, "They always do, Bill."

I wish the sun was out. I like to watch snow melt. That's my new hobby.'

October 22 – Needles – to Manly

Snow. Pretty scary when a truck goes upside down 4 km. above the scales. I put up pictures of Larry's accident with 'Order your Depends now' just to keep these guys scared. Barnes Road has 1½ feet of snow. Roads are bad.

June 17 – Snag Bay – to Manly

Our loader-man, Mighty, visited the Kos' crew logging up the hill from the sort- yard.

The bucker said, "What a long drive!!! (*Grand Forks to Snag Bay to work)*
Mighty asked, "Where are you from?"
The logger said, "Quebec."
Mighty replied, "Yup, that's a long drive alright…no wonder you are tired."

February 29 - Stobo - letter to Manly

(I left home at midnight for the scales. Early shift meant trucks could haul while the roads were frozen and before they thawed and became muddy about noon.)
It's 3:00 a.m. and I have already done more loads than you will all day. I said to the loader-man, Mighty, "It's cold this morning."
Mighty said, "No, it's going to get cold." At 1:30 a.m. the coldest part is yet to arrive.
I love these new hours – I've heard every woman's a 10 at 3:00 a.m.!

February 13 - letter from Manly

The tug is sitting down there with the bilge alarm going off. I'm waiting to find out where the key is so I can go and check it out. There is a little water in the bilge but nothing serious. The loader-man went over, turned the alarm off but wasn't sure what to do so turned it back on and sat there listening to it.

February 6 – Stobo - letter to Manly

What's new? Nothing. A trucker gave me a newspaper only 10 days old but I was too busy to read it on Thursday and someone stole it Friday.
That's a major disappointment.

THE FUN STOPPED

Manly was transferred from his usual scaling site to one he'd never worked at before and told when the regular scaler returned in a few weeks, he would not be permitted to return to his original position.

This came soon after he reported dishonest scaling. It was after breakup, months later, he was told he would not be rehired. Our on-the-job banter ended.

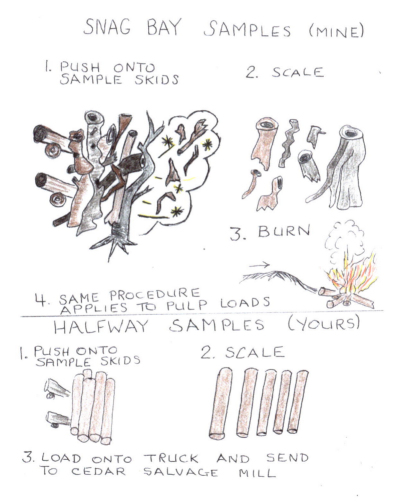

A cartoon was sent to Manly comparing sample loads at my scales at Snag Bay to his at Halfway scales.

Beauty and **brains.**

And, oh yeah, a healthy measure of **brawn.**

MATERIAL SAFETY DATA SHEETS LIST SAFETY PRECAUTIONS AND HAZARDS FOR WORK SITE PRODUCTS. e.g. SPRAY PAINT

OUTHOUSES

Nik will be remembered for spending long periods of time in the outhouse. As truckers waited, they schemed, and I overheard their plan to wrap a cable around the outhouse and hoist it into the air with Grunt's self-loading logging truck. I knew they were capable of such mischief but fortunately for Nik, I was assisting him scaling that day and the truckers did not have to wait for his appearance.

A loader-man asked Nik, "Why don't you go to the bathroom at home when it's two hours out of your day here at work?"

Nik replied, "Why, when I can go on company time?"

The cartoon was inspired after a dynamite blast from road construction damaged the Octopus scales outhouse.

WHO STOLE THE OUTHOUSE?

In 1980, I worked at Needles scales when trucks delivered logs from a Lumby sawmill. The huge inventory of logs had been decked at the mill yard for too many years. These deteriorated logs dumped in the sort yard for me to scale shattered into a billion pieces. The loader at the Lumby mill yard was extremely slow but there was a constant line of trucks so many trucks waited up to five hours for a load. The Needles loader-man, Don "Hazard', was also not popular; one Lumby truck suffered a bent reach and two loader-fork punctured tires in one day.

Truckers were waiting at the scales hours ahead of me in the morning. The first trucks back to Lumby had the shortest wait for a load so there was an eternal race for first. Beer cans by the scales suggested a way to pass the time.

Judging there would be a break between trucks, I made a frantic dash for the outhouse only to stop very bewildered. Wrong trail? No…. the outhouse had vanished.

Okay, I could take a joke. I expected the old shitter to be sitting on the weigh scales when I arrived at work in the morning but days passed with no sign of it.

A co-worker radioed our supervisor at the CanCel office with the following message on the occasion of the disappearing biffy, "Lois has been sitting with her legs crossed for days so please hurry and take her an outhouse."

Finally, as the Lumby truckers were about to quit hauling, I made pointed questions about the disappearance of the shitter but only received strangely blank looks.

Years later, I discovered it was local loggers who scooped the outhouse and relocated it at their campsite at Whatshan Lake. Larry figured I would receive a new replacement and they would trade up some night. There was disappointment at Whatshan Lake when my 'new' outhouse was a decrepit and smelly relic.

PRESERVE WILDLIFE...
PICKLE A SQUIRREL

MOUSE SANDWICH

March 7 Stobo scales

I was entering the previous day's loads by timber marks and strata by hand on Forest Service forms while my cheese sandwich heated in my toaster oven. I smelled something but thought the cheese had melted onto the element. Oh, no! It was burning fur! There was a mouse leaping at the toaster door. How horrible! I opened the door and he fell to the floor with singed whiskers. This is inhumane and disgusting.

I gave him my sandwich to help him recover but he is not eating. The boss picked up a shovel to <u>kill</u> him, but he ran under a piece of plywood. The boss picked up the plywood so he could <u>kill</u> him, but I screamed, and Mr. Mousie ran to the junk corner. He's alive!

Just then Dirt walked in and said, "It smells in here. Are you cooking a mouse?"

He recognized the smell because he explained he likes to microwave them and watch them blow up. Disgusting. He must have read the children's book, 'POP goes the Hamster and other Fun Microwave Games.'

SCARY WILDLIFE

I was not bothered at all when a sow grizzly and two cubs passed within a few meters while I was feeding my herd of chipmunks. I was not concerned by black bears in apple trees while I was scaling or even with a black bear running out from under the scale shack when startled by a logging truck. Although the pack rats stunk and it wasn't nice of them to chew on paper and wiring, I could relocate them with a live trap without fear.

BUT... in a submission to a Forest Service scaling newsletter, I wrote:

'Today is a scorching hot May day, but we're talking <u>cold-blooded</u> critters. And it's scary! Charlie, the tape holder helping me measure log lengths, never heard me scream. Honest! I simply refused to measure the logs a monstrous snake was laying beside. Charlie shooed it under the logs so I could tape them. Arrgghh. But I did it!

Charlie remarked it had a fat tummy and had probably just eaten something. No kidding, is that why the last scaler is missing?

Oh, no! Tomorrow is forecast to be another scorcher and I have diameters to measure on that load. I offered another scaler the job but he must be afraid of snakes so I should not have mentioned the monster was as big around as my arm, was the same colour as cedar bark and probably not native to Arrow Park.'

(I did finish scaling the infamous load, but I quickly measured diameters standing up on the logs as I spooked at strips of cedar bark.)

SAD MARTEN

Manly discovered a marten wallowing in the outhouse hole at Fosthall scales. He set a long thin pole down the hole so the marten could escape from the deep and semi-liquid slop. The miserable marten wandered away leaving a stinky, brown trail through the snow. He muttered and chattered in obvious disgust. The marten paused, and according to Manly, looked back and said, "Thanks, man."

RODENT FRIENDS

I fed chipmunks and Columbian ground squirrels ('gophers'). After our absence from Snag Bay for almost a year, ground squirrels showed up immediately for a handout.

Heading home one afternoon, I spotted something on the road and asked Bear, the loader-man, to back up. A very young ground squirrel was lying unconscious with a hairless mark on his forehead. I took him home in my lunchbox. He remained in a coma until the next day when we began to feed him milk in a small syringe. Unfortunately, he stunk as only a rodent can, and, as I was cleaning his cage, our dog killed him.

Baby Columbian ground squirrel emerged from coma from road accident.

Columbian ground squirrel at Snag Bay

CHIPMUNKS

At Needles scales, the chipmunks ran up a large bill for sunflower seeds, but the entertainment was worth it. They traveled great distances from all points of the compass to cram their cheeks with seeds and scurry away. After a rain, caches of sunflower seeds sprouted all over the sort yard. We tried to count how many seeds two cheeks could hold – A LOT! One had a fright in the scale shack and POOF! His cheeks emptied and sprayed seeds across the floor.

One weekend, to my disgust, a trucker caged the friendliest chipmunk to turn loose in his trailer park. I can imagine the screams of terror when this critter was trapped when no chipmunks trusted coming for their seeds on Monday.

ROAD WARRIOR - MARMOT

As I made the rounds feeding ground squirrels at Snag Bay, I noticed a unique scruffy marmot missing most of his tail. He often hung out under the parked pickup. One day, he somehow traveled fifty kilometers in the undercarriage of the pickup and disembarked at the loader-man's house in Edgewood where he had quite a tale to entertain his new friends.

SQUIRREL FATALITY

January 23 - Needles

Truck number 280 had a squirrel go through the fan and the driver described, "CHINK, CHINK then no- go."

COUGAR COUNTRY

Many hours were spent traveling through cougar country seeing tracks and cougar-killed deer carcasses. As I walked by the Snag Bay scales, the loader-man (Mighty) saw a cougar following me. I had despaired at ever seeing a cougar and had just complained as such. I should have turned around!

FLICKER

Hauling a load of logs down the hill to Snag Bay, coffee cup in hand, a driver had a flicker fly in the open window and begin pecking him. A flicker has quite a beak but is not generally known for attacking people!

BEAR STORIES

These two stories circulated about dead bears:

The first bear was found dead in a hollow cedar tree and was placed in a load of logs destined for the sawmill. As time lapsed, the deceased bear grew more pungent. Apparently, the sawmill crew was not impressed.

A trucker, Bob, confessed to antics that transpired during a bout of wine drinking with companions. It seems the grader operator was not popular with them, so a dead bear cub was set in the grader seat and adorned with the grader-man's vest and hardhat. A hot three-day weekend did neither improve the odour of the bear cub nor the disposition of the grader man when he reported to work.

RATS

Pack rats often invaded the scale shack. I live-trapped and relocated them some distance away.

After rats chewed and urinated in a box of Forest Service paperwork, I innocently labeled the box as 'bio – hazard' with a warning of 'rat pee'. I never foresaw the uproar when the check scalers delivered the mail to the office.

RADIO - WHERE ARE YOU?

As a Forest Service dispatcher, I used formal radio protocol. Certified identifications, or call signs, were required by the senders and receivers of all messages. A radio log recorded times, call signs and the conversation.

As a scaler, I learned logging radios were essential but leaned toward informal. Call signs were not used: "Where is the loaded truck on Barnes?", "Empty 3 k Octopus", "Leaving Fosthall scales".

Haul roads are named e.g. Worthington, Barnes. They are numbered every kilometer from the start of the road. Truckers radio 'up 9 Octopus' or 'empty 9 Octopus' as they return for a load of logs. If they hear 'down 12 Octopus' or 'loaded 12 Octopus', a safe place is found to pull over so the loaded truck can safely pass.

WHERE ARE YOU?

The radio offered some chuckles. When Ivan was asked what road kilometer he was at so trucks could meet safely in a known location, this conversation often ensued:

"Ivan, where are you?"

Ivan's response was often, "R – r-right here."

HAVE A HEART

Initially the weigh scales were not equipped with radios. Working in isolated locations with no radios in the pickup, loader or scales could be a concern, for instance when the loader-man complained for months of heartburn and I feared it was angina.

My supervisor said, "Wait for a truck if anything happens", but that would mean up to a three- hour wait.

Flat tires were common occurrences, but the loader-man refused to let a woman help change tires. What a scary situation for me as his pain noticeably increased while his chivalrous nature refused my assistance! He made it to the end of the job before undergoing heart surgery.

HOW TO GET A RADIO

A trucker was hit in the head at Snag Bay sort-yard when a log fell off his load. A logging crew started down to the sort-yard in an ambulance upon our request but was unable to radio and notify us their vehicle had broken down. We were out of radio range for contacting the office for a helicopter rescue, until a forester arrived on scene. I remember clearly the two and a half hours spent in the muddy and snowy sort-yard with the patient on a spine board while we waited for a helicopter. I knew from paramedic training how vital it was for the patient to receive prompt medical care and fearfully watched for his condition to decline. I also recall two hours of the patient's conversation as he partially regained consciousness and repeated continually: "Did I f*** up? Is Dale pissed at me? Did I wreck the truck? Did I f*** up? Is Dale pissed at me? Did I wreck the truck?" The log dump loader-man missed all the excitement and as I clued him in with the day's events, he said, "There's nothing you can do for an injured person but give them Tylenol." I was too emotionally exhausted to argue.

Fortunately, the trucker survived his concussion and broken bones.

From then on, the scales received good radios, safer log handling procedures were implemented and improved first aid equipment was available. Latitude and longitude locations became imperative so a helicopter could easily be directed to a location.

Although the Company never extended kudos for our efforts, WorkSafe did on numerous occasions.

SUCKERPUNCHED

GOING TO DUMP YOUR LOAD IN THE LAKE?

As a loaded logging truck leaves the scales, a loader-man often queries if the load is destined to the sort-yard or to the log dump at the lake.

Jordy was on the scales weighing a D8 cat to check if his low-bed's highway weight was legal.

The loader-man, Frank, watched and radioed, "Are you going to dump it in the lake, Jordy?"

GOOD NEWS OR BAD NEWS?

We heard a grader owner, Russ, talking on the radio to the mechanic trying to fix his grader, "Don't talk to me unless it's good news."

The mechanic responded with, "I might not be talking to you again."

MUDDY BREAKUP ROADS

The radio was busy with chatter about the adverse (uphill) 3 kilometers above the scales. March had brought spring thaws and the soft road was trapping trucks in the mud. Truckers were whining endlessly on the challenge of navigating the deep ruts. The Needles loader-man asked if he should take his loader up and pull the trucks through the mud.

There was a brief silence after this comment made the radio waves, "Breakup is like sex. If it gets soft and you can't get it up, it's over" until someone responded with, "Only for a few minutes."

DON'T TALK SO MUCH!

The radio channel was essential for road safety, but a few talked too much. I said of one Cherryville trucker who babbled endlessly about nothing, "Some people can talk for hours on any subject. Some don't need a subject."

QUICK CHUCKLE

A logging truck driver, Darwin, radioed the sort-yard loader operator, "Frank."

Frank responded, "What do you want?"

Darwin: "Not your body."

Frank: "Well, you never know."

SHORT DISTANCE RADIO RANGE

Commonly, a radio call was heard on a radio with farther-reaching reception than the intended recipient. One day, a trucker said I was being called but I could hear nothing on the scale shack radio. He offered to relay the message to me. To our astonishment, the transmission originated from the sort-yard only a few hundred meters away and confirmed the ineffectiveness of his radio and the improved efficiency if the loader-man merely yelled messages.

FUNNY OR RUDE?

November 18

I turned on my logging frequency radio this morning. Yesterday there was constant complaining over chaining up logging trucks, slippery roads and snow. A small snowfall could make a big difference and today someone said, "I can live with one inch."

A second person said, "One half inch is too much for me!" and I just had to respond, "Not for me." Gar was laughing when he drove on the scales with his load of logs.

A Needles loader-man often responded to a radio call radio with a ditty.

CBC RADIO DOESN'T CUT IT!

A logging truck driver and I rode home from Snag Bay with the loader-man. The trucker warned the driver we would probably meet a low-bed truck hauling heavy equipment at the 17-kilometer sign and commented on the fact our pickup had no radio. We therefore could not communicate with the low-bed driver to choose a safe spot to pull over in advance of our meeting.

The loader-man contested not having a radio and announced, "Yup, we got a radio."

He then turned the AM/FM radio to CBC static for the duration of our drive. Much to the loader-man's surprise, we narrowly missed crashing into a low-bed on the 17 km. corner.

When he was finally given a radio for the pickup, he was ecstatic. His joy persisted even though the radio remained behind the seat, unconnected.

ODDS AND ENDS

I WAS SAVED BY A GUARDIAN ANGEL

HERO'S INCREDIBLE UNTOLD STORY OF FAITH & COURAGE

"My guardian angel kept me alive!"

'I was huddling with my face in the dirt — I could sense an angel by my side & I heard him tell me: I am with you, I will protect you'

They were followed by a man who was herding the animals.

He went through a deeply religious experience and was "aware of a protective presence with me."

DM meets cougar eye to eye and bashes the furry critter with a stick. Environmentalists are in an uproar. When asked what it's like to confront a cougar, DM replied, "Smell my pants." "The worst part", he said, "was confronting my wife who bashed me with a stick on my arrival at home after hearing I had been after a little pussy." DM has recovered from the cougar scare but still has scars from his wife attack.

This cougar incident occurred as DM was walking a block of timber scheduled to be logged. A cougar stalked him so closely, DM did hit it with a stick.

'Scaler's Weaklies' were collections of jokes, my cartoons, photos with goofy captions and often re-purposed newspaper headlines. 'Cut and paste' meant glue and scissors in pre-computer times. Copies were distributed to the loggers and check scalers. Laughter is better when shared.

When a Vernon logging truck driver wondered if there really was a cemetery across the road from Needles scales, I affirmed, "Yes, that's where I bury the truckers who piss me off." The look on his face was one of shock, knowing at that point I was rude, not just a sweet little thing.

A deer paused on Octopus scales when the workload was minimal. The cartoon vulture was a reminder for employees to keep moving.

SUCKERPUNCHED

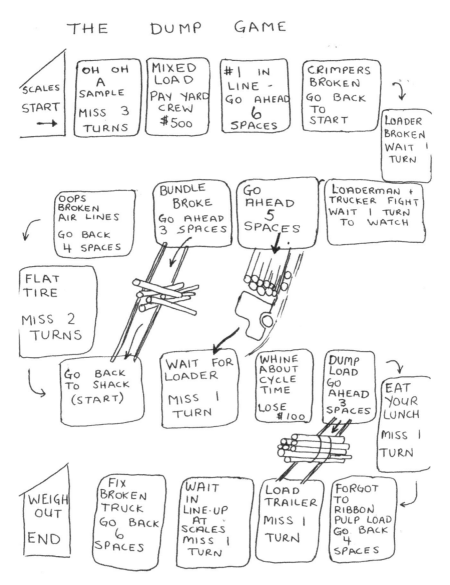

Tony saw me designing this Dump Game and said I was totally cracked/looney tunes/nuts…this from someone who offers me a beer at 5:00 a.m.

CHRISTMAS SONG

Hark! The bush angels sing,
"P+T have taken away
Our skidders, trucks, quotas and jobs
And given themselves a raise in pay.

They've given us an old donkey
For all of us to earn the dough.
So this Christmas you will see
Us on our ass in the snow.

Weighing an empty at Snag Bay scales. (Somewhat smaller than the usual weighing of an empty logging truck.)

This was offered as a suggestion for new improved cut blocks to combine logging and anti-logging. Messages, or pay-to-log ads, would give cash to loggers.

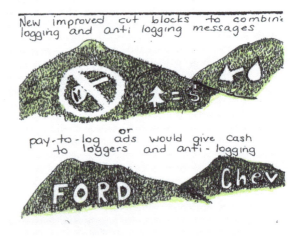

At times, Snag Bay disasters were rampant. In one week, three feller-bunchers rolled, a logging truck crashed and even our company pick-up had five flat tires.

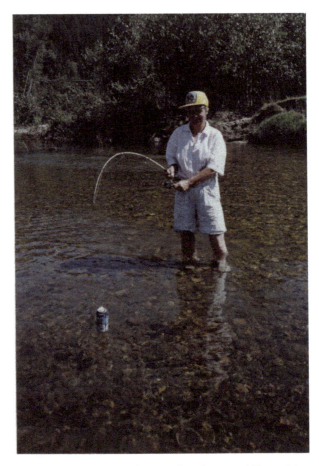

Especially after hauling his last load on a Friday afternoon, Mike anticipated relaxing on his houseboat and fishing for kokanee. In reality his houseboat was on dry land in his yard and the "kokanee" was canned beer. Borrowing Mike's idea, I produced and sold postcards to support a local animal welfare organization.

GOOD MORNING SNAG BAY!

One week left. I've heard that for months. There are skidders and trucks broken down every day. When Toby's yarder was slow finishing, they gave Dean more blocks to log so there would be more than Toby's two loads daily. Then Toby finished but Dean isn't. I figure now they'll give side 1 more to log until side 2 is done, then side 2 will be finished and side 1 won't be so they'll give side 2 more…..

Top view is of descending Johnston face to Snag Bay on the Arrow Lakes
Bottom picture shows logging cut- blocks along the Arrow Lakes

Scalers enjoyed a trip to the Castlegar sawmill and pulp mill and seeing how chip trucks are unloaded.

UNDERWATER TUG

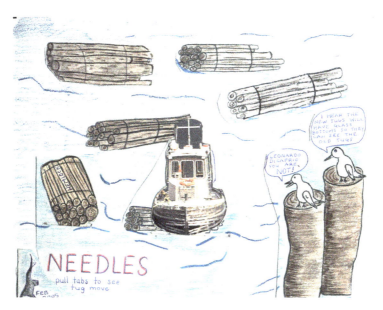

One morning at Needles log dump, only the antenna on the roof of the tug showed above the water. The boat crew scrambled to a log bundle and awaited rescue from a small dinghy from the Needles ferry. This cartoon had pull-tabs to pull the tug underwater and flaps to lift up to see what was under the log bundles.

VIEW FROM NEEDLES

ON REFLECTION

On reflection, there were good people who made it easy to enjoy my job. I was offered rides to work at 4:00 a.m. and home after work when the system of scalers riding to work with the loader-men failed. Often, I arrived at the scales anticipating a big effort clearing the snow off the scales only to find the truckers finishing the work. I remember an abundance of laughter, candies, new jokes posted on the wall and happy faces drawn on the log ends.

'Sometimes I laughed so hard, tears ran down my leg.'

A bumper sticker given to me said: 'Hug a logger, you'll never go back to trees'.

Some of the best years of my life were immediately followed by the most challenging times.

PART 2

A Year in the Life of a Victim of Workplace Violence and Post-Traumatic Stress Disorder As Recorded in my Journals

I did witness decades of injustice, knowing that an employee would be fired without cause, for reporting dangers in the workplace or for receiving Worker's Compensation for injuries.

Fortunately, I kept a journal. Most entries are bare bones brief. Some days I could not handwrite and only a painful struggle to complete a few words remains. At times, writing was possible when coherent speech and cognitive skills failed.

I have kept the following in chronological order.

Much later, I philosophized over my ordeals having been preventable and deliberate.

FRIDAY, SEPTEMBER 6
THE ASSAULT

As the hot summer mellowed into September, the two loader-men and I were enjoying a carefree break from the monotony of work. Activity at the scales was slowing down and this was Seemore's last day at this site. The anticipated weekend brought lightened spirits and laughter. I had known Lars and Seemore for thirty years; we shared a no-slack diligence to get our work done…and appreciation for a rare time-out.

Slugger was the most obnoxious trucker we encountered. A self-proclaimed know-it-all with an offensive attitude, his first load of the day spoiled this day's elation.

Slugger operated a self-loading logging truck and was paid by volume for loading. Dry lodgepole has more volume per tonne than green wood and the difference could mean $20 per load more. He harassed scalers by trying to have a load of green wood called dry.

Whenever I determined that his load did not meet 'dry' specifications, Slugger confessed I was correct but that I was allowed a 10% error. He never relented and dragged me by my coat to re-inspect loads while he pointed out dry logs. My responsibility was to scale loads correctly.

Slugger returned on that infamous Friday. Lars, our sort-yard loader-man, was in the scale shack as I inspected Slugger's load. Lars barely endured Slugger's particularly miserable disposition when he voiced his annoyance as I inspected his load, "You'd think the money was coming out of her own pocket. I should dump the load in the sort-yard, so she has to hand scale it."

He also complained that he should go to other scales with his loads. Lars just shrugged his shoulders and said, "Go."

Usually I retrieved the weigh slip from the printer when truckers weighed out but this time Slugger walked over and took it. I was puzzled when he said, "You are lucky or you'd be extricating my boot from your a**hole." He signed the weigh slip, set it on my desk and I received an unpredicted violent blow to the side of my face and blacked out. I did not regain consciousness until Slugger was long gone. A hit and run.

Still dazed, I foggily went outside to the two loader-men and said, "I wish Lars had stayed in the scale shack. Slugger hit me."

They said I was holding the side of my head and asking if my face was swollen. They commented on my strange behavior as being hysterical with a strange giddy laugh.

When I later complained to Lars that my cheek was stinging like stinging nettles, he confirmed I had been hit. When I next saw Seemore a month later, I said, "I know I talked for hours after the assault, but I have no recollection of what I said."

Seemore remembered me holding my face and saying non-stop, "My cheek hurts. It stings. It's not right to hit someone, is it? My cheek hurts. It stings. It's not right to hit someone, is it?"

REPORTING A VIOLENT ATTACK

I was shaking and sobbing as I reported the incident to my employer. Boss asked, "Were you wearing your hard hat?", and I replied, "I was sitting at my desk."

He added, "Slugger does not work for me; this has nothing to do with me."

Boss referred the matter to Seagull. By then my face was red and swollen. Seagull said the Company could lay charges against Slugger on my behalf and added, "If I had a bottle of whiskey, I would go to Slugger's house with a baseball bat and I am surprised you have not sent someone there with a gun."

Slugger's employer told me, "I asked Slugger what happened today, and he said, 'Nothing'. When I asked if anything happened at Needles, he said, "No."

I asked if anything happened between Lois and him and his answer was, 'Oh, I patted her on the arm and said, 'Have a good weekend.'"

I replied, "Slugger hit me, and it was WAY more than a slap."

Slugger's employer then said, "Then Slugger is gone." He would haul the next workday at Meadow Creek, off the Tree Farm and three hours from my worksite.

Seagull said the employer was told Slugger was to be fired.

Slugger was, in the words of his employer, a very 'busy boy' after the assault phoning everyone he could to say I was 'setting him up' when all he did was 'pat me on my head', or 'tap me on the shoulder', or 'touch me on my arm', and say, 'Have a good weekend.'

These actions were prior to his employer or the timber company confronting him in regard to an assault.

Monday September 11

SLUGGER RETURNS/ RCMP VISIT

From the scale shack, I saw Slugger's truck on the ferry and was terrified. I had been assured that he would not appear. I panicked; I paced on the road until I could flag an empty truck down and ask the driver to stay with me. He had commented on my swollen cheekbone when he weighed in loaded. Support came from a big, burly man able to carry a side of beef over his shoulder who shielded me from overwhelming terror of Slugger. I never stopped crying.

PARK YOUR TRUCK, SLUGGER!

I was uncontrollably shaking and bawling. I had 300 logs in a lodgepole sample to scale and was trying to write diameters on the logs, but I was crying so hard I could barely see.

Boss said it would be good for me to keep working. Why am I here? Why won't he send someone to work so I can go home?

I phoned Seagull to ask if I could tell Slugger not to come back and was assured he was ordered to park the truck.

RCMP REPORT

I had not stopped crying when I decided to phone the police so I could sign my name to a legal document stating the truth about the violent assault.

The constable was quite a distance from me (ten meters) as I walked toward him and he said, "Right cheekbone. You don't have to tell me where you were hit."

His words were golden when he added, "I believe you."

I had a written statement prepared for the RCMP. The officer offered to deliver a copy to the Company.

A friend had spoken to this RCMP officer a few days before and repeated how the company told me they would lay charges on my behalf. The auxiliary cop present was not surprised with Slugger's violence; as a logger he had experienced serious confrontations with him.

Tuesday September 12
EMOTIONAL DISTRESS

I find I am dropping things and at times feel like I am losing my balance.

I spent hours in emotional distress; Usually, I'd be outside with the pretense of scaling but mostly just crying.

A forester stopped in for my written statement and I said RCMP had already taken it to the Company office. I asked him if he'd heard what had happened – he said third hand – so I told him.

I was sure the truth would be accepted and brighter days were coming after the company held a meeting regarding the violent assault. I believed justice would be served by my employers. I had a passable night as far as getting some sleep. *(Addition: ' and the last one for weeks.')*

I determined that Slugger is a sick puppy and I was just a victim.

Wednesday September 13
FIVE DAYS AFTER THE ASSAULT

When a woman, carrying a camera and a clipboard, came to the scale shack, I thought she was there to investigate the attack. She wasn't. She was studying the location for a local Internet tower.

She did offer to take pictures of my obvious facial injuries.

A Vernon trucker arrived at the scales. I explained my crying with, "A trucker hit me." He immediately said, "Your right cheek; I can see it."

I phoned Boss and said my face was still bruised and swollen and noticeable to five people not being prompted where I had been hit. A meeting regarding the assault was being held at the Company office the next day. I thought visual proof of the assault was important information to bring up.

The company receptionist called on company business. I said my face still has visual signs of a hit. She replied, "You have a reputation of a lot of credibility".

Thursday September 14

Boss told others the incident was Slugger waving a load slip at me and giving me a love tap.

I phoned a scaler to say, "Six days after the assault my cheek is swollen; it was a severe blow; I didn't cause it. I wanted to tell you the truth and warn you Slugger is dangerous."

She replied, "Oh, it can't happen to me."

Six Days After the Assault
COMPANY MEETING

The Company held a meeting regarding the assault. I was not invited to attend but was confident the incident would be dealt with appropriately.

FRIDAY SEPTEMBER 15
COMPANY DECISION ON VIOLENCE

At 1:30 p.m., the Company Manager phoned. When asked if my boss had called with their verdict after the meeting, I said, "No".

He said, "Slugger was not invited but he showed up and we allowed him to speak. Those present decided it is 'He said, she said' so the consequences are a cooling off period of separation wherein he cannot haul to your scales and after that it is business as usual".

I was devastated. I am a victim – in two weeks I cannot work because Slugger can come back to my scales and I cannot accept that. I have spent days in fear that he will come to my house. I don't know why he hit me. Now I have reported him to employers and RCMP, he could be really angry and want to hurt me a lot worse.

I told Company Manager, "That is not acceptable. I talked to the RCMP and made a statement. Slugger was arrested and charged!"

Company Manager stated that he had not talked to RCMP.

I asked, "Did Boss report that my face was still swollen five days later, and five people had picked out my injury site with no prompting?"

Company Manager replied, "No."

I never ever considered I'd be a victim of a violent attack by a co-worker. That'll leave a permanent scar by itself. I spent this week in constant fear. I was 'gun shy'; I flinched when anyone moved at the scales. I even jumped when I thought I felt movement behind me. My mind is not functioning at a normal level.

The employers' decision devastated me. In horror, I phoned a friend.

She advised me to phone WorkSafe who said they don't deal with my situation. Maybe I wasn't clear to them what happened.

I called WorkSafe again to ask if I am to report injuries on the job and she said, "Yes", so I asked her to mail me forms.

I was a total wreck Friday night. I called friends for support.

Who was punished over this incident? ME. I was so naïve thinking that by telling the truth there'd be justice. The violence in itself is difficult to deal with. There was enough evidence for the police to press a criminal charge of assault in a workplace, yet my employers aren't even recognizing it.

The people I was counting on to help me, to support me, to believe me, to protect me, to serve a judgment befitting the crime against me all destroyed me by making a decision without seeing me or speaking to the RCMP.

My mental state since September 8 has been a roller coaster – extreme lows then up-hills. Certainly, I have never experienced so many tears, fears and feelings of such failures of my beliefs in people and justice and on and on and losing my job because of a crime committed against me.

I was not sleeping well, not eating much or properly, and going around zombie like with no drive or energy or will.

A check scaler phoned. I told her the verdict of assault by the company. I was so appreciative of that call because at that point I felt no one cared. I was really distressed. She had witnessed a scaler showing up for work, "She was a MESS. Slugger had beat her and hit her in the face."

Saturday September 16

MENTAL BREAKDOWN AND HOSPITAL EMERGENCY

I went to the Farmers' Market but was barely able to think or function. I was stumbling around, blubbering and babbling. I just cried and cried.

Friends were concerned about Slugger coming to my home and suggested I keep a hammer by my bed, but I was afraid he would grab it and use it on me.

Friends recognized the signs of a mental breakdown so referred me to a nurse who ordered me to go to the hospital. I wept during the hour's drive, wailing that I should tell my employers to see me in a total meltdown: 'You saw Slugger. Come and see ME.'

I was uncontrollably bawling at the nurses' station. I could not answer the nurse's questions and did not know what a Care Card was. A doctor hustled me to a bed in Emergency.

When I began to explain my history to the doctor, he immediately said, "WorkSafe forms are required."

When asked if I had been unconscious, I said, "I don't know. All I remember is 'Blam!!', my head went to the side and everything went black".

The doctor said," You were unconscious", and ordered head x-rays.

He gave me a note for 2 weeks off work, and I was to see a counselor. He said, "This is negligence."

His order to stay away from work brought relief. My brain was a mess.

Saturday September 16
A CHARGE OF ASSAULT

The RCMP called to say Slugger was charged with assault. He lawyered up and said nothing to them. I get a no-contact order for two residences and Needles scales. The RCMP said Slugger's actions after his arrest indicated guilt when he neither acted surprised nor denied the charge.

I bought two dead bolts so my house doors would lock from the inside. I also bought bear spray. There was no reason for Slugger to hit me; it is reasonable to figure he could do it again; WE ARE NOT DEALING WITH LOGIC HERE.

I was given sleeping pills at the hospital but am too afraid of taking anything that decreases my consciousness. It's the fear that Slugger could come here at night.

I take aspirin or Ibuprofin for my headaches but that's all.

DOCTOR ORDERED MEDICAL LEAVE

I called Boss and said, "I have a doctor's note to take two weeks off work."

Boss asked, "What's this about?"

I repeated what I said and asked if he wanted a copy.

Boss later publicized that I was only taking 'stress leave'. In fact, my condition was not labeled when the doctor told me to take time off. I interpreted the abbreviation 'F.U.' on the note as 'F---ed up' which made sense at the time. Months later so did 'Follow Up'.

Sunday September 19
ACHES AND FEARS

My cheekbone aches like the dull pain following a dentist visit. 9 days after the big blow by Slugger

Sunday night was tough – I was so afraid to go to sleep. Gary will install deadbolt tomorrow!

September 20

FIRST SUGGESTION WHY VIOLENCE WAS NOT RECOGNIZED

Appointment with doctor. He wants weekly visits.

IMPACTS AND FEAR OF NO PROTECTION AT WORK

Doctor said no one fired Slugger because of fear of being sued. So. No one came to see me; it's me protecting myself. Am I messed up for life? This is not a broken finger that can heal without pain and scars. So, I feel my employers have really let me down. Now I am supposed to go back to work: business as usual. I am afraid. It's been what? 12 days? I'm a bloody mess; do they know, do they care? I think caring would've happened by now, like a personal visit. Slugger made it easy for them – not much to deal with if they believe his lies.

I realize now I should not have stayed at work after the attack – no one asked if I'd be okay to work so I tried to tough it out. Crying hours every day. Again, I guess this was lack of support from employers. Boss should have come down and replaced me. I can't just leave when there's no scaler on site. I realize how ineffective my brain was.

September 21

A LITTLE HINT OF A BRAIN

Boss has not called. He has not shown compassion; he never came to see me. I don't have brain flashes… more like pssst – little fizzle but brain starting to work a bit.

My sister said if day- by- day doesn't work, try hour- by- hour, even minute- by -minute. I wonder if tough people like me crash harder when they finally lose control of themselves than people who are 'weaker' who don't fall as far before they are defeated.

THE NAME OF MY CONDITION IS PTSD

My counselor gave me an article about post-traumatic stress disorder but at the time, I was not capable of reading. It was a major achievement after weeks of tenacity when I was able to read and comprehend a pre-school reader.

Elated, when I understood the PTSD article, I realized, "Hey! This is me! My condition has a name: post traumatic stress disorder!"

Page 7 jumped out – behavior of others at or after incident… ostracism by management, co-workers….

Wow – I have the majority of symptoms etc. I am still shaking, heart racing, am near tears and it's been 13 days!!! Trying to talk to a friend tonight – she said I'm disoriented. I forget what I start to say, etc. If it weren't for friends, where would I be now???'

I am not a typist and my brain was totally befuddled, yet I miraculously copied the article about P.T.S.D. with no typos on an old typewriter, adding the correlation of my experience. The brain works, or doesn't, in mysterious ways.

I gave it to my employers to explain how the assault and lack of employer support affected me. I never received any response. Did they not understand or just not care?

POST-TRAUMATIC STRESS DISORDER

I am the victim of an assault. While sitting at my desk, without warning, I received a blow to my head and blacked out.

> 'MOST OF THE EVENTS IN OUR LIVES ARE EVENTS FOR WHICH WE ARE RELATIVELY PREPARED AND ABLE TO MANAGE. AN EVENT THAT GOES WELL BEYOND WHAT WE EVER MANAGED TO FACE THROWS US INTO A SPIN. THESE EVENTS ARE CALLED PSYCHOLOGICAL TRAUMA OR, IF THEY OCCUR IN THE WORKPLACE, CRITICAL INCIDENTS. A TRAUMATIC EVENT IS A JOLT TO OUR PSYCHOLOGICAL SYSTEM. IT IS AN EVENT EXPERIENCED AS SUDDEN, UNEXPECTED, INCOMPREHENSIBLE,

SHOCKING AND PERSONALLY UPSETTING POTENTIALLY RESULTING IN EMOTIONAL AND PHYSICAL TRAUMA.'

After the assault, I had no thought process and no sense of reasoning. I was stunned. I was in an altered mental state, was incapable of recognizing that and incapable of knowing I was in need of medical attention and should have reported to WorkSafe and R.C.M.P.

'NUMBNESS, DISBELIEF AND SHOCK ARE NORMAL REACTIONS TO TRAUMA. THEY SERVE TO PROTECT FROM EXPERIENCING THE INTENSITY OF THE TRAUMA.'

My beliefs in telling the truth, feeling safe at work, job security, trust in co-workers and believing my employer and job-site company would care for me were destroyed.

'FACTORS THAT AFFECT THE SEVERITY OF THE REACTIONS TO A TRAUMATIC EVENT INCLUDE:

- SEVERITY AND NATURE OF THE INCIDENT
- DEGREE OF PERSONAL DANGER
- DEGREE OF PERSONAL IDENTIFICATION WITH THE INCIDENT (e.g. KNOWING THE ASSAULTER), THE GREATER THE POTENTIAL IMPACT
- BEHAVIOUR OF OTHERS AT THE INCIDENT OR AFTER THE INCIDENT CAN MAKE IT WORSE (INCLUDING OSTRACISM BY MANAGEMENT OR CO-WORKERS).'

'WHEN AN INCIDENT OCCURS THAT WE BELIEVED WOULD NOT OCCUR, IT CAN BE VERY SHOCKING AND DISRUPTIVE. "IT WON'T HAPPEN TO ME" BECOMES "IT CAN HAPPEN TO ME". CONCERNS THAT IT COULD HAPPEN AGAIN, FEELINGS OF FEAR, HELPLESSNESS,

> VULNERABILITY, LOSS OF SAFETY AND SECURITY OCCUR. WHEN INNOCENT PEOPLE EXPERIENCE A DEVASTATING ACT, THEY CAN FIND THEMSELVES QUESTIONING THE MEANING OF LIFE OR THE FAIRNESS OF LIFE. AT TIMES, IT CAN CHANGE CORE BELIEFS ABOUT LIFE.'

In my reduced and altered mental state, I believed that by reporting the incident, that co-workers, employer and job-site personnel would care for me, protect me and support me. No one ever came to see me. No one guided me to assistance. I felt absolutely abandoned. The person who assaulted me could return to my work site. Fear of my attacker meant to me the loss of my livelihood. I was disturbed that by doing nothing to help me, my employers were delivering a message that violence in the workplace was acceptable. That, combined with the trauma of an assault, caused me to suffer post-traumatic stress. That has affected me physically and mentally. I changed from an athletic, academic and full of joy of life individual to an incoherent, fearful, confused, forgetful, crying, physically and mentally weak person unable to complete a previously simple act of washing dishes or comprehending a book.

Almost a month after the incident, I am on a slow and painful road to recovery. Medical personnel, R.C.M.P. and friends have supported me. To assist myself in therapy, I decided to write this letter to hopefully prevent further unnecessary post-traumatic stress victims.

I cannot simply bounce back to work, 'business as usual' with no recognition that I sustained a life-altering incident and no preparation to improve work-place standards and safety.

> 'WE DO NOT SIMPLY 'GET OVER' TRAUMATIC EVENTS. THESE EVENTS CHANGE US.'

> 'SOME POSITIVE LEARNING CAN COME FROM ANY TRAUMA e.g. HOPE, STRENGTH, LEARNING, GOALS, GROWTH. FINDING THE POSITIVE LEARNING HELPS US TO MANAGE THE PAIN IN THE HEALING PROCESS.'

My hell with post-traumatic stress could have been reduced or possibly prevented by appropriate actions by my employer. Policies and procedures for trauma victims should be in place to offer immediate help and support.

Being a victim of a violent assault is a terrible tragedy. Being a victim of subsequent post- traumatic stress disorder amplified by lack of compassion, support and protection is unforgivable.

(The quotations are from: TRAUMATIC STRESS – Sources, symptoms and solutions Written by Toby Snelgrove PhD)

The following is an excerpt from:

> TRAUMATIC STRESS: Sources, symptoms and solutions
> Written by Toby Snelgrove PhD
>
> ADVICE TO ORGANIZATIONS
>
> If a traumatic event occurs in the workplace:
>
> 1. Provide trauma defusing services to your employees immediately after the incident and debriefing services within a few days. These services have a tremendous impact on employees' healthy recovery from a traumatic incident. They also build morale through the demonstration that management cares for their well-being.
>
>   For those most seriously affected, provide access to a professional counselor trained in trauma counseling. Employees should not be provided time off without the provisions of these services.
>
> 2. In all cases, make sure you have clear policies and procedures on trauma in the workplace and that all your employees are familiar with sources, symptoms and solutions of traumatic stress.

September 22

REGULAR DUTIES AT HOME WERE UNACHIEVABLE FOR WEEKS

Washing dishes was almost insurmountable; I would fill the sink with water and aimlessly wander away. Later, I would drain the cold water, add hot water and drift away. It was a major accomplishment after weeks of futility and determination when I could finally complete the task.

September 23

WHERE DID MY BRAIN GO?

Went to feed the cows. Forgot the hay. 9:30 p.m. and I think I forgot to eat.

My brain and body move in slow motion and I cannot hold a thought.

'I WILL do this today' was soon lost as I wander away and complete nothing.

Can't get dryer to work – forgot to close door. Washed clothes on Friday. They were in a laundry basket on the kitchen floor, but I didn't notice until Tuesday so just rewashed and hung out.

A commitment to fill a trough for the horses with a garden hose and then turn the tap off, failed. I tried wearing a coiled plastic bracelet as a reminder of the duty. I determined that I would stay by the trough until it was full. The pasture became a virtual lake every time

A friend visited and I decided I should make tea. In super-slow thoughts and movements, I thought, "I guess I need water. And a kettle? Oh. Tea bags. I wonder where they are? And cups? Where are cups?"

I'd get a thought to do something and then have no idea seconds later what I was going to do.

Weird. I go outside. Think I should trim horses' feet. Oh, maybe put garbage cans away. Maybe rake the yard. Or stack firewood. And I don't start anything.

I have no strength. And why was I wearing felt-lined winter boots on a hot day?

Friends all say I'm not speaking coherently yet I thought I was doing okay except for forgetting what I was talking about or having blank spots.

When talking or writing, I totally lose my train of thought and can't think of names or appropriate words.

I pour myself a glass of milk and then can't find it.

I cannot multi-task and don't seem to get anything done or finished.

But I started to realize how screwed up I was. I must've been really bad!

My thinking process was severely affected. E.g. calling WCB/RCMP/doctor never entered my mind.

EXPENSIVE WATER WITH MY MEAL?

I ordered supper at the local Legion and then was asked what I wanted to drink. I said, "Water, please," and when the reply was, "Ten dollars," I stood befuddled for an interminable length of time while I slowly contemplated the price of a glass of tap water, 'Maybe they are charging for water now, but I think ten dollars is quite a lot.' I'd temporarily forgotten about ordering supper. Slowly I thought 'maybe it was a joke'. When they laughed and repeated, "Ten dollars for one supper," I understood. This is so weird having an empty head.

A trucker at the Legion told me Boss says they are waiting for the police to make a decision. I feel a meltdown coming on.

PREPARING FOR A HIKE

I decided if I slept the night before, I'd go on a hike with an outdoors club that had been planned for months. I inwardly questioned what clothes I should pack. Should I take a Gore Tex jacket in case it rains? If it's cold, I may want a warm coat, or maybe a fleece vest or a wool vest but maybe rain pants or snow pants. Gloves. I should take gloves but light or heavy ones? Spare socks? I could not make choices, so I completely filled my Supercab pickup with clothes. I may have discounted the importance of packing food, since I usually forgot to eat anyways.

I have no recollection what I packed in my backpack.

In hindsight, the other hikers waited an intolerably long time for me to complete the hike. I made it to the top of the peak; could that be significant?

WHAT IS $10 ?

At a store till, when advised to pay $10, I opened my wallet but had no idea what a $10 dollar bill was. I should have said, "No understand English," and handed the clerk my wallet.

CARDBOARD NOTES

I often booked appointments to Nakusp on Fridays so I could use the government Para-transit bus. The schedule has remained unchanged for years and leaves for the return trip at 1:50 p.m. My note was on cardboard and I looked at the 1:50 notation every 5 minutes to check my watch.

MY JOURNAL ENTRIES OUTLASTED MY MEMORIES

I've decided to write everything down. Then try not to talk about this incident except to pros. It's wearing me down. I have CRAFT: Can't Remember A F---ing Thing.

SHOCKED VISITOR

I was trying to prune small branches off cottonwood trees, knowing a day with PTSD accomplished less than an hour's normal work. I shuffled slowly like a 90 year old and kept losing my balance. A Forest Service check scaler arrived for a visit. Her greeting was not a cheery, "Hello", it was a shocked,"Oh, my god!"

I did not clue in; I thought I was doing better! As a former violence victim, and present at the scales when her co-worker arrived 'in a mess' from a facial beating from Slugger, she later spent an hour explaining the impact of violence to my boss. Nice when someone shows they care and think I was wronged.

INSOMNIA

My insomnia is not waking up often. It is never sleeping at all. How many weeks can I go on like this? Still awake at 1:00 a.m. when I heard one horse whinnying for the other horses. I was hot, opened window, covers off, covers on, coughing. Not much sleep! Shaky, uncoordinated. Feel like I'm going to lose my balance.

Thinking about episode drains me more. Why hasn't Boss called me since September 11? Why has he never asked how I am doing? Where did the month go? I thought it was middle of month and there's only a week 'til the end. Writing feelings down has always helped. I'm beginning to understand how serious, unprovoked and insanely violent the act was. Then the more I see that, the enormity of my employers not showing concern becomes.

I WILL OVERCOME THIS!

I am still uncoordinated – find myself losing balance and stagger.

Lost 3 pounds. Ate at a cafe at noon – soup and bun. Then I should have eaten tonight, just never got around to it.

Bought myself a card: 'Brighter days are coming. Who knows? This might just be the first one.'

Even though I tell myself I can overcome this, I can see it's major. Not going to be easy. When I said a roller coaster, ups and downs, it's more like a ball hitting the bottom and bouncing up just a wee bit. But when you hit the bottom of the well, the only way to go is up. But.. I think I was at the bottom and guess what, I wasn't, I go lower. But I still have some ups! One day I will go high enough to get out. I feel like a struggle to climb even one bit takes an overwhelming determination and saps my strength. I make a little bit of a climb up and then I get knocked down to the bottom. It is so hard to try again. It seems so futile.

Tough to lose the belief that truth will win but I must have hope it eventually will. How wonderful to have friends. They definitely outnumber the people who have let me down. They do pull me up the well and keep me from crashing way, way, way down.

Good at my job? Yes. I also LOVED my job. How lucky I was to have a job close to home, I loved and was good at.

IMPORTANT THINGS IN LIFE ARE NOT THINGS

Yesterday my doctor asked if I had any thoughts about hurting myself and I said, "No, that is not me." I'm thinking how much I do love LIFE. How I usually work hard because I like it – clearing 25 acres of logging slash by hand, brush-sawing 20 acres of dense cottonwoods, cleaning up new properties, spending time with my horses.

I have never been a lover of money – my love has been the simple things in life.

So, hurray! This is so HUGE to release more crap out of my head. Being on the top of the mountain on Sunday may be significant. Now I know it was the sheer delight in experiencing the basics (nature's blessings) that is important.

Suicide may be a consequence of PTSD. I did not think I would consider it even at my lowest point. A chilling thought was if I took that step, those responsible would not be held accountable. I refused to allow employers to 'win' at that level.

September 27
PHYSICAL PAIN FROM INJURY

My mid-jaw up through my cheekbone aches. And I have a headache above that. I have not had a good night – not much sleep.

Very much like pain from dentist – achy. It's been three weeks. I've had to work hard at concentrating to get one thing done.

OCTOBER 1

Today I feel overwhelmingly SAD. Just SAD.

I am losing the will to fight. Is that what is counted on?

October 3
MENTAL AND PHYSICAL PAIN

So much pain in right side of my face. My sinuses feel like they are draining into my throat, ears plugged.

OCTOBER 4
WHY DOES BOSS NOT BELIEVE ME?

A friend took me to my counselor appointment and explained I was abandoned after trauma.

I hear from many that Boss figures I am setting Slugger up if all he did was pat me on the arm and that I claimed compensation for nothing.

My counselor agreed I did everything on my own - phoning him for appointment, going to emergency, doctor, RCMP, Victim Services. I said to my counselor, "It's too bad my boss won't spend one hour with you to learn what I am going through".

October 6
WORKERS COMPENSATION SUPPORT

WorkSafe phoned. They have counseling available after an incident. Oh Boy, it feels good to have someone ask how I am doing and for me to talk.

My doctor does not want me to return to work until safety concerns are met.

OCTOBER 12
ANXIETY TRIGGERS AT SCALES?

Wondering if I'm asked to explain what the blow felt like – I can't say like being hit in the face with a 2x4 because I never have been. Words… what words describe it? Sudden, felt my head fall to the side, a hard blow.

I got a letter from Joyce and tried to write back but it takes me too long to write so I gave up. Those days are a lost cause.'

My counselor suggested I return to the scales after hours to learn what 'triggers' adverse emotional responses. My heart pounded rapidly like a bunny rabbit's and my anxiety elevated soon after leaving home. I persevered and entered the scale shack. On the wall, almost leaping out at me, were Slugger's load slips hauled during the two- week Company ban and the Court's No Contact Order for Needles scales. Those should have meant recognition of the assault and concern for my safety. My feelings? Betrayal and the realization support for the victim were not forthcoming.

When I asked Boss how Slugger would have known immediately after my request for medical leave, he casually said, "I told him. I said it would be fine to haul to Needles and he did until his lawyer advised him it was not a good idea with an existing No Contact Order from the Court."

The logging area Slugger hauled from was midway between Needles and Stobo (Arrow Park) scales with the convenience of Stobo being far closer to his home. Although my Boss seldom spoke to me after the assault, he did to my assailant on many occasions.

BOSS OPPOSES MY CLAIM FOR COMPENSATION

WorkSafe said they had the Employer's Report of Injury and Boss declared that Slugger and I were arguing on weighing in. What? Lars was there the whole time – we were not arguing. Why is he trying to get my claim denied?

Trying to clean up house – company coming. Very slow - keep losing balance. Sweating – yet it's 65 degrees in here.

October 13

GRADUAL TESTING OF THE WATERS?

Had 2 sleepless nights Tuesday and Wednesday.

My doctor will ask WorkSafe about me easing back to work. He suggested trying one hour or so at first. My right cheek still feels 'heavy' and stuff draining into my throat is now thicker.

EMPLOYER TO MAKE A SAFETY PLAN

Boss phoned. WorkSafe wants him to draw up procedures if a worker is expected to be in danger. He asked them, "A camera?" and they said, "No."

He then asked them, "Radio, phone, loader-man?" and they replied, "Not exactly."

Boss does not understand what they want. I said, "I sent you a letter pointing out what happens with PTSD and how I needed medical help after, but I was in shock and did not know that. My assault should be separated from what is needed for safety procedures and violence prevention.

Slugger gave me no warning, no cause. He is crazy. There is no logic in what he did."

October 14
RARE CALL FROM BOSS – WHY AM I NOT AT WORK YET?

Boss phoned and only asked about me working next week. I answered, "My doctor is going to talk to WorkSafe about my easing back to work. It's not up to me to say when I return, it's up to doctors and WorkSafe."

2:12 a.m. Can't sleep. I cope not too badly until I think of going back to work then I am terrified with memories of being hit and so much lack of support from Boss and Company. Sometimes I get so profoundly sad. At 3:24 a.m., I went back to bed. Can't sleep. Have to get up and cough up crap – seems to drain into throat and just sit there – doctor doesn't laugh."

October 17
7pm MELTDOWN – NO COURT?

Phone call from RMCP Constable. Crown Council is not going ahead with charges. There was not enough argument that would lead to me being hit. I am a total wreck. Friend said to phone my counselor at home. My sister said she could be here in 3 ½ hours.

A radio station telephoned asking for an interview, but I declined, crying that I would be fired if I spoke out.' From my altered, mixed up P.T.S.D. mental state shone a bright beam of truth. In reflection, either choice would have had the same result. The reporter reacted to my hysterical sobbing:

"You are a mess."

I had been so sure that honesty would come out in Court. Slugger would have to get on the stand and tell the truth. The violent assault would be proven. The Company and Boss would know what happened and la- la-la everything would be fine.

Wrong. A criminal conviction for assault means proving beyond a reasonable doubt. Slugger would not have to get on the stand. Even truth is not a sure thing in Court.

The violence was a knockout punch. Workplaces, even Civil Court (balance of probabilities), do not require such stringent parameters as Criminal Court. I waived my right to sue in Civil Court to WorkSafe who then had the right to recover costs from Slugger.

October 18

PAINFUL SYMPTOMS

(*writing in diary obviously strained)

I thought September was as low as I could get. Boy, was I wrong. And I have this damn sinusitis?? And I have sweat dripping from head to toe. And I have steady headache that doesn't respond to aspirin or Ibuprofen.

Have appointment with doctor at 11 a.m. Got antibiotics –cheek has been sore since September 17. I get sweats. Right now am freezing cold. Nose isn't plugged. Right side sinus still drains into my throat.

October 18

ONGOING SUPPORT FROM MEDICAL TEAM

I spoke to my counselor. In regard to Crown Counsel's "If there wasn't an argument, they can't see why Slugger hit me", my counselor said, "None of us can." He cannot believe how I have been treated; said it's like I've done something wrong. Yah! That is how I feel.

October 20

FIRST VISIT WITH COMPANY MANAGER

I went to Company Manager on my own initiative. Almost a month and a half since the incident and the first time he has seen me. WorkSafe and Boss never have. I was shaky and timid but determined to present the truth of the violent attack. I offered my personal diaries for him to read and permission to discuss my case with my counselor but received no reaction.

He said he would not pay for two scalers for me to ease back to work and see how I cope. I badly wanted to remind him of the months two scalers were paid at slow scales just so one would not be laid off. The Company Manager stated Slugger will continue to haul to Needles and he cannot be treated differently than any other trucker. He said my Boss could not arrange his life to be on 'standby' if I had a panic attack.

I went to my doctor appointment. I sat in the waiting room for over an hour where my doctor saw me, said I had the wrong day, but took me in anyways. So much for thinking I could do without notes.

FEAR OF AN ATTACKER

How can I deal with this fear of my attacker in a logical manner when there was no logic, no reason for the attack? I was violated. I lost trust in a co-worker, trust in a safe workplace and trust in support and protection by the companies. There was no remorse, no truth, no empathy shown by Slugger. I was knocked- out by him and he walked away. A hit and run. An accident can be accepted and dealt with. A deliberate cold-hearted blow to the head done when I wouldn't see it coming is insane.

October 23
PAIN AND DEPRESSION

What is the reason for pain in right side of my face? My sinuses now feel like they are draining into my throat, ears plugged, right nostril dripping a bit. Not exactly like a cold. (* Is this change (draining) after doctor prescribed antibiotics?)

I feel better at times then fall into depression again. Still not great memory, don't lose my balance as often. I am so discouraged. Wonder how I can handle fear (terror!) at facing Slugger. Seems like I lose, lose, lose for what he did. Will I ever be like I used to be? Happy? I am tired of fighting. I am tired of letdowns. I am tired of no energy, no thinking power.

I called the Crown Prosecutor. Criminally, they need to prove beyond a reasonable doubt. Had I called his load 'green' there would have been 'cause'. She explained that Slugger is NOT innocent just because charges were dropped. Criminal charges are strict, serious with NO doubt. She added it was a heinous crime and he is likely to re-offend. She did extend the length of time his file is open from 2 to 5 years.

BACK TO WORK SPECIALIST

Met with WorkSafe's back to work specialist, Lulu. I said, "Fear is not keeping me from going to work at Octopus, it's forgetfulness. I have to have notes for everything.

I am afraid to drive to Nakusp because Slugger lives near this office."

Lulu laughed at my terror when I saw him drive past the window. These people just don't get it. Lulu said my doctor wants a gradual return to work for me. I said my employers won't pay for two scalers. My WorkSafe claim is pending. I said I passed my psychiatrist report on to my doctor in which he determined I had PTSD compounded by lack of employer support.

Later, I repeated the details of the meeting to a government enforcement officer who said I should not have gone alone. I had been subjected to an interrogation technique wherein the questions suddenly shift from describing the assault and planning a back-to-work strategy, to random inquiries about my relationships with siblings and the schools I attended. I had trouble holding my train of thought and was annoyed at these ridiculous questions. I did not understand quickly changing subjects causes inconsistencies in accounts if a person is lying. I thought Lulu was simply a 'back-to-work' advisor but she was probably testing the validity of my statements. She annoyed me but her test proved my truthfulness.

PTSD IS FOREVER

Will I ever 'get over' PTSD?

I will never be the person I was before the assault. I lost trust in honesty and justice. I tend to avoid contact with people. I lost laughter. Daily, I work myself to exhaustion hoping I can beat nightly insomnia or nightmares forcing me to flee my bed at 3:00 a.m. I wake in a cold sweat from dreams that Seagull or Boss or Slugger is in my bedroom. I awake from dreams I am at the scales and Boss is laughing and calling me stupid because the computer is changed and I am confused. I dream I am hitting Slugger with a stick and he just laughs.

I cannot return to bed: I sew until daylight and escape to the outdoors and clear brush or work in my garden.

I now recognize my bravery in refusing to be defeated against overwhelming odds and cruelty.

> 'When things are bad, we take comfort in the thought that they could always be worse. And when they are, we find hope in the thought that things are so bad, they have to get better'. *Malcolm S. Forbes*

And I added – 'and when you think things can't possibly get worse… they do'

BACK TO WORK
WORKSAFE COMMENDED ME FOR INITIATING MY RETURN TO WORK.

Employer decision: Slugger was not to be treated differently than any other trucker therefore I was not permitted to return to Needles scales. He suggested I stay home without pay.

This decision did not address the danger of violence Slugger presents to other workers. The assault on me was never mentioned or considered. I believe my employers' hope was I would shut up and go away; without accepting the assault, there was no problem and no errors in their (flawed) judgments.

BACK TO SCALING WITH IMPOSED HARDSHIPS

I initiated my return to work. I desperately needed to know if I could master log scaling again.

I was offered work at Octopus scales expected to last five months. Even when WorkSafe and doctors recommended I begin with a few hours a day to check if I was healthy enough to cope, my employers refused to support that.

My doctors were amazed at my initiative to return to work but hoped it would accelerate my healing. My diaries confirm how far from well I was. I heard so much adversity from my employer about the costs of having a compensation claim, I subconsciously feared having all future employment terminated.

I would have to satisfy WorkSafe I had my own safety plan should Slugger return to my worksite, knowing I had zero support from my employers. I now know my determination overcame immense obstacles.

October 27
QUESTIONING MY WELLNESS

At my counselor appointment, he said I had a concussion and it can take a year to recover from PTSD. I followed all the indicators and steps of PTSD. I have been strong which accelerated my recovery process.

I commented, "The past 6 weeks have been hell!"

My counselor commended my strengths, "Many people would have taken a year to accomplish what you did in 6 weeks."

I had a doctor appointment. Forgot my note but remembered all by myself.

I bought a locking chain for the Octopus door a.k.a. piece of plywood. No phone there.

I phoned Boss and said I could go to work on Monday.

He told me how screwed up the computer was:

'It's um uh the scaler has to um power it off and um uh um sometimes um 3 times and uh.'

I asked what kind of computer is was and he said, "Toshiba."

I said I'd had one before.

Boss: "No, um. This one is um different. Maybe the loader-man can help you."

The loader-man had never touched a computer before.

I do not think Boss believes me about the assault and PTSD. Maybe I was not well enough to consider work. I am not sleeping.

October 29
NO SLEEP AND EMPLOYER RUDENESS

No sleep last night. Concerned about computer set up at Octopus. Boss will be away. I phoned Seagull early Sunday to ask if he could be by the radio the next morning in case I had problems with the computer.

I said I hadn't slept at all last night. He said, "You should have had a young hunk in your bed to f--- you all night, and you should go down the street and f---k (this person) and (that person). He added, "You are strong. I cannot believe your mental powers were diminished. Just get over it. This incident is news from Vancouver to Prince George."

In tears, I phoned a friend who advised me to report Seagull's remarks.

I called Boss, who laughed and said my supervisor didn't remember saying that. I contacted the head of the company who admitted my supervisor had a history of such behavior. The result was a notice that I was not permitted to contact any company personnel after hours.

I called Boss later and said, "Slugger has put me through hell. If you have any doubts, I will try to arrange for my counselor to talk to you. All through my statements I see how I wanted the truth told. Slugger is scary. Even the Crown Prosecutor put a five-year note (from two) on his file because he hit me with no warning or provocation and just walked away and she considered he would re-offend."

OCTOBER 30
OCTOPUS OPEN UNTIL BREAKUP... FIVE MONTHS

I went to work at Octopus.

The Octopus loader-man advised, "I have seen on TV that's how victims are treated so just get over it."

A large table leg sat on my desk with 'Slugger's' name added to it by Octopus truckers. Thanks, guys!

Boss phoned at 5:30 pm to see how my day had gone.

I said Slugger could assault me, knock me out and probably didn't even get a disciplinary letter. Boss replied that there was nothing he or I could do.

I said, "I hope they re-evaluate it, it's me paying the price and I am a victim. I would give them permission to access police, counselor etc. files for evidence."

October 31

OCTOPUS SCALES SCHEDULED TO CLOSE

News today was the logging contractor is going to pull out of Octopus. The loader-man suggested I could scale sample loads at Needles. I asked Boss if I could return to Needles for that. He gave me a definitive 'NO'. Why am I being punished?

I asked Boss if he had read my statement of the assault, but he's been too busy to read it.

November 3

WORKSAFE SUPPORT

Chris from WorkSafe phoned. He commended me for moving forward and acknowledged I have had a tough time. He wants me to go for a neuro-psychologist assessment. He could have chosen just psychological exam, but my concussion may be a factor so wants a neurological assessment as well.

The WorkSafe psychiatrist accepted my claim as normal PTSD.

I said, "Finally someone is talking to me like I am a person."

Chris replied, "Well, you are."

Thank you!!! I then slept for 11 hours!!! He saw a person behind the claim.

November 11

A WARNING FROM MANLY

I talked with Manly who was terminated as a scaler after reporting dishonest scaling. He said they will try to set me up so I quit or….

November 14

NO ANXIETY OVER A CRASH

I was with the loader-man in the morning when our truck crossed lanes on an icy highway corner and crashed into a concrete barrier. I never got anxious. My first action was to warn oncoming ferry traffic of ice and the blocked highway.

November 15
TWO WEEKS, NOT FIVE MONTHS

Not a meltdown but I feel almost near tears. Last day for bush hauling for Octopus – tomorrow clean out sort-yard, then what? Out of work?

Boss phoned – leave computer at Needles when I am done. He said I have $1384.20 in vacation pay but I have to take time off to collect it.

November 16
OCTOPUS CLOSED UP

Octopus cleaned out/ shut down. Seagull said I have to stay away from Needles until after breakup (six months).

Like my counselor said, I'm made to feel like I've done something wrong.

Two loader-men said, "You shouldn't have reported it – look what it did to you."

November 17
LAWYER SUPPORT

I am not working.

My lawyer said, "Employer has an obligation to treat you fairly. Now that Octopus has shut down, they must make different accommodations for you. It is not reasonable to endure 4 hours travel to Fosthall as a result of being assaulted. It would not have happened if you had not been assaulted. Your employer has an obligation to provide a safe workplace."

November 20
FOSTHALL SCALES

My first day at Fosthall scales. I talked to a Needles ferryman. Maybe if I am on the Needles side at 4:40 am I will get across. Otherwise I wait for

5:15 ferry. (Ferry going from shuttle service to schedule at Needles) I was home at 5 pm.

November 22

Left home at 4:20 am.

Lawyer said employer in the wrong for not removing Slugger from work site. Extra travel equals a demotion. Slugger should have been removed from work site, not me.

November 29
NEURO-PSYCHOLOGIST ASSESSMENT

Appointment with neuro- psychologist in Nelson.

Sister went with me to hear assessment results. I asked the doctor about my behavior following the assault: 'giddy laughter'? and periods of amnesia and he said I had been traumatized and had a concussion. My sister asked him if they would ever get the 'old' Lois back and he said, "No. She'll be changed."

The results of neuro-psychologist assessment: 'not yet over PTSD' and that was after a month of back to work. Sister and he came to same verdict: I am (now) timid.

Friends and doctors all see me differently than I feel. I think I am doing almost fine/normal, they say, "NO!" Am I that far away from used-to be? Am I still so screwed up?

November 30
FOSTHALL LOADER OVER SNOWY BANK

Left home at 4:15 a.m. for Fosthall - 10 inches of new snow and roads not plowed. Loader went over the bank, home after 7 p.m.

Made another request for company email from October re reporting Seagull's rudeness resulting in my not being allowed to contact personnel after hours, and also for my holiday pay.

December 1
I'M TO GO TO SNAG BAY

I am being sent to work at Snag Bay.

Boss left the Snag Bay computer in my truck at Arrow Park. I looked in the computer case – why did Boss disconnect all the cords, (power, printer and modem etc.) and the mouse and leave in a jumble in the case? Never done before – they are left on the desk in position to simply plug into the computer. No pay for 3 months and cheque shows $2398.27 withheld with net pay as $802.61.

December 4
SNAG BAY START

A trucker watched as I opened the computer case and saw all the cables tangled together, and he said, "Someone worked hard at that."

Carbon printer paper put in backwards and other 'mistakes' setting up the scales.

A forester came to Snag Bay. He said Company Manager did not know how to deal with the incident. (I suggested he could have asked for help.) The forester said it was Seagull who was the root of the problem.

When I said Seagull had been telling me that he was the only one who believed me, the forester just shook his head. He said Seagull has drinking problems. I didn't know that when I phoned him about being by the radio when Octopus started.

I thanked the forester for talking, said everyone is avoiding me like I have the plague. He told me I am a victim. (So why do people tell me that like it's okay and accept it?)

The forester said he told Seagull he wouldn't help him on the job anymore – drinking makes him rude with sexual innuendos. He said if I need supplies, I can phone him. I explained why I could not call after hours although I have not seen copy of email yet.

December 7

SNAG BAY

Handheld computer will not download samples.

Propane heater will not stay going.

DECEMBER 11
FIRST MEETING WITH BOSS SINCE ASSAULT

Boss came to Snag Bay to fix the propane heater. THE FIRST TIME HE HAS SEEN ME SINCE THE ASSAULT THREE MONTHS AGO!!!

Finally, I had my time to speak.

I described the assault. He said he never read the statement I wrote after the assault. I explained to Boss what PTSD episodes were like and he said, "I didn't know it was so bad."

He knew another female employee was hit by Slugger but added, "Oh, but she didn't work for me for long after."

Boss was really uncomfortable during the conversation over the violent assault.

He sat in a corner, hunched over in his chair with arms clutching his chest and I would describe it as 'cowering.'

I got a WorkSafe letter in the mail!!! Hip, hip, hooray!! Boss phoned and said he had the dates we'll be off for 'summer' holidays. (I corrected him, "Christmas.") Scales close noon 22$^{nd.}$

He sounded really uncomfortable and was stammering. He asked if I had gotten a letter from WorkSafe because he just got one. I said, "Yes".

The envelope did contain the approval of my compensation claim and the documentation supporting the decision. Boss was opposed to my claim.

December 16

REQUEST SEPT 14 MEETING MINUTES

Mailed letter to Company Manager asking for copy of "statement' Slugger made at the meeting on September 14 regarding the assault.

December 22

RECEIVED MINUTES OF SEPT 14 MEETING

Got requested letters from Company Manager —minutes from September 14 meeting and memo re. me not contacting any company personnel after hours.

MINUTES OF MEETING

> Arrow Lakes Timber Division
> #507 Scale Incident (September 8)
> Meeting Minutes – September 14
> Present: Company Manager, Company Forester, Slugger, Slugger's employers, Lois' Boss

1. 'Slugger's statement: We were all involved in a practical joke.

2. Lois stated green stratum, obvious dry. It would take a lot of beer to change stratum. When he got the ticket, it was printed "dry". Slugger patted Lois on arm and stated good joke, have a good weekend.

3. Company Manager asked Slugger if he had ever harassed another scaler? Slugger said no.

4. Slugger stated he has always had a good relationship with Lois and does not understand.

5. Slugger's employer called Slugger Friday night and asked him what went on. Slugger was surprised anything went on.

6. Slugger called Lois (also Friday night) and asked what happened. Lois said I hit her.

7. Slugger's employer was able to reach Lois on Friday night, she said she did not know how he hit her, but stated 20 minutes later her cheek still stung. Lois admits playing a joke on Slugger. Stated he always argues about stratum. Slugger's employer

told her to charge him and take it all the way or it's hard to do nothing.

8. Slugger's employer stated Lois always wanted to be one of the boys.

9. Boss stated that Lars and Seemore both said when she came out of the scale shack, she said Slugger hit me.

10. Boss phoned Lois on Sunday and gave her the option to go to Renata. She said no and says Slugger can haul somewhere else.

11. Boss said scalers have the final say on stratum.

12. Slugger left the meeting at this time but asked for a copy of the notes.'

MY REACTION TO THE MEETING MINUTES

Neither my written statements, nor my obvious injuries were considered. Those present at the decision-making did not see me after the assault and before the meeting. They did not conduct interviews with my co-workers. They did not check out Slugger's statements with the loader-man present at the time, although he would later sign a statement for me that all were false.

Boss had not seen me or discussed the incident with me. Three months after the violent assault, Boss said he had 'not had time to read my statements'.

Tonight I am angry.

December 24
VERIFYING THE TRUTH

I wrote out excerpts of meeting minutes that Lars was witness to and he signed that Slugger's statements were not true.

January 2

Seemore said he was getting fuel in Nakusp in September when Slugger approached him and asked if Seemore would talk to his lawyer because he was in a lot of trouble.

December 28
PLEADING TO BE BELIEVED

I sent a copy of my WorkSafe file, which included medical reports and their decision to accept my claim for PTSD, a concussion and facial trauma, to Company Manager. I included Lars' statement verifying Slugger's comments made at the September meeting about the assault were untrue. I wrote, "Here is proof I was assaulted. Please revisit your decision."

January 21
COMPANY POLICY MANUAL

I received a letter from Company Manager, attached was policies manual.

The Company Manager wrote:

'Thank you for sending the WorkSafe information. In your letter you refer to a September 14 decision. I am not aware of a decision made on that date that was related to your situation.

I have enclosed a copy of the Company's workplace conduct, that applies to all of our employees and our contractors.

It is best if you do not work at Needles scales until after Spring breakup.'

RUDE AWAKENING

Now I know truth doesn't matter. Did Slugger threaten them? Why is my punishment supposed to last nine months after the violent attack? The Companies' workplace conduct and policies deal strict consequences for harassment and violence but apparently not in my case. Why?

January 22

I phoned the Grand Forks Human Relations manager who wrote the manual the Company Manager sent me.

I said, "In the policy manual, it says the incident will be investigated but no one ever came to see me."

HR rep: "It was your employer who did the investigation on my behalf."

I said, "He did not see until December. I want people to realize I am telling the truth and now I have proof from WorkSafe."

HR rep: "WorkSafe does a thorough investigation. You got your lost time paid for."

January 23

REQUEST FOR REVIEW OF MY WORKSAFE CLAIM

I received a letter from WorkSafe. Boss requested they conduct a review of my claim. Appears it's not about me as much as about money – Boss wants Slugger's company to pay the $4200 bill for my compensation.

January 27

Was Boss requesting a review of my claim or a review of his bill?

Says he disagrees with decision because:

    a) 'employee was alleged struck by another company's employee

    b) The trucking company should pay claim costs.

    c) He said, she said. Is in RCMP and Crown hands.

    d) Possibly, if can would pay the compensation fee.

    e) Boss has very safe record and is having much difficulty with results that WorkSafe has concluded.

    f) Employer would have kept employee working and away from alleged other employer's employee if she had desired.'

Are the objections to my WorkSafe claim totally monetary? I think so. I am so discouraged.

The phone call from the Company Manager on September 14 giving the results of the decision made over the assault sent me into a major tailspin. One medical report says I suffered two traumas: #1 the assault and #2 the failure for employers to support me. And I am still going through hell… and what is it? Five months later!! Why NOT do a revisit of their September meeting? Why not set a precedent that violence will not be tolerated? Why not conduct an investigation? Thoughts of how wrongly I have been treated overwhelm me pretty much 24/7.

February 11

HEALTH AND SAFETY REGULATIONS FOR ALL WORKERS

An oil sands safety executive lent me B.C. Occupational Health and Safety Regulations. Had those been followed, I would have received the help I desperately needed immediately.

She said employers have to remove danger. I should refuse to weigh my assaulter and refuse work in a dangerous workplace. She is so upset nothing has been done for me.

Boss said to WorkSafe in an obvious attempt to stop my claim:

Slugger and I played a game. (I AM A SCALER. I DECIDE WHAT STRATUM HIS LOAD IS)

He said I wanted Slugger fired. (WRONG. SLUGGER'S BOSS AND SEAGULL SAID HE WOULD BE FIRED; I ONLY SAID I DIDN'T WANT HIM HAULING TO MY SCALES.)

He said Snag Bay is my normal rotation place to work. MY DIARIES FOR THE LAST THREE YEARS SHOW I KEPT NEEDLES.)

Boss said to WorkSafe he made numerous calls to my home and work. Glad I keep diaries. He hardly ever called.

February 18

QUESTIONING MY LACK OF CARE

Manly stopped in. Asked, 'How does it feel to have no one care?"

I said, "Care? It is in my mind 24/7 – not so much the assault but how I have been treated. Unbelievable – I have stacks of paper verifying what happened."

The disclosure package from WorkSafe is an inch thick.

February 22
DEMAND FOR MEDICAL APPROVAL TO GO TO NEEDLES

Boss phoned.

He has no problem with me going back to Needles but my WorkSafe case manager said I should have doctor approval before going back to Needles.

I said, "The neuro-psychologist said it would be a good idea if Slugger and I were at separate scales. He meant Slugger should have been removed from Needles. Not me. If someone shoots you, they don't put you in jail.

Also, if/when I go back to Needles, Slugger can stay in his truck – he can put his load slip on railing and get back in his truck. He can sign the load slip after I am back in the shack."

Boss discounted the suggestion with, "Slugger may not like that."

I countered, "Well, tell him to go to the RCMP and complain. No one has supported me in this at all. It's time they did.

I read the minutes of the September meeting. I wish I had seen them after the meeting so I could have defended myself. Was my statement read out? Did you mention my face was still noticeably bruised and swollen five days after?"

Boss said, "No."

I continued, "When Slugger's boss asked me what happened, he said, "If he hit you, then he's fired and if he hauls for someone else on the Tree Farm License, then I'll sue the timber company."

Even though there was a no contact order to keep Slugger away from my worksite, he still hauled there."

Boss defended Slugger's actions, "You said you had a doctor's note for two weeks off."

I asked, "How would Slugger know that?"

Boss explained, "Because I told him. Slugger hauled to Needles then his lawyer advised him not to."

I stated, "No one has supported me – maybe it's time they did."

Boss avoided my concerns with, "Well, we'll deal with that if you go to Needles."

Sister phoned – my lawyer has papers. Call lawyer immediately if I get laid off at Snag Bay and don't go to Needles. Sometimes I feel like I shouldn't have sent my lawyer papers then another little voice in me says, 'No, it's a good thing I have someone with me, backing me up. Sister says I have a loaded gun in my holster. I know I felt stronger talking to Boss because I felt I had power.

February 23

BOSS WANTS MEDICAL ASSESSMENT BEFORE NEEDLES

Message from Boss:

He allegedly found a letter from my WorkSafe case manager who wants me to go to a doctor for assessment before going to Needles.

A friend said, "Good. Boss is sending you to Needles, then he has a responsibility to protect you i.e. make Slugger stay in his truck (You are being easy only asking for that.) or keep him away.

All my pleas to present the truth to employers about a violent workplace assault and subsequent post- traumatic stress disorder have been ignored. Why?

Are they afraid? Did my attacker threaten them? They held my life in their hands and turned me away. I feel violence in the workplace was shown to be acceptable behaviour.

Was how to care for employees after a violent attack, prevention and understanding of critical incidence stress and P.T.S.D. learned and understood? Or was the lesson solely to pretend nothing happened and hope future victims go away?

Workplace policies and procedures should be complied with or they are just so much paper. I have met a large number of employees fired for reporting violence or hazards in the workplace. How many have to die because fear of losing their job overcomes their right to report dangers?

I suppose I thought they cared. The truth is they did not care about me. This has been a tough life lesson to learn. My life is not inconsequential. I did survive; many would not have.

February 27

HOPE AT SNAG BAY FOR EMPLOYER SUPPORT

Snag Bay. Received Boss' letter re. to return to Needles, I need doctor's note of approval. Seemore read it and responded, "It is crap. No one can do a better job than you."

Boss is not even doing safety meetings.

Boss has seen me one time in six months.

Slugger knows he got away with the assault: no repercussions. A friend said I might think Slugger would never hit me again, but she is not so sure.

Nor, a Company forester, came to Snag Bay. I said the precedent set is that violence is okay. Truckers feign a punch and say, 'My load is dry logs.' Nor was shocked by that. I don't care; they would not hit me. They know Slugger got nothing for assault so it means they support me.

I said, "Between you and me, it's not so much fear to ask that Slugger stays in his truck, it's to ask one small thing and see if my employers will support me. No one has yet."

Nor said he would talk to Company Manager. WOW!!!!! He said only 2 days before he was reading that hysteria or 'laughter' (i.e. me after being hit) is a key symptom of ---darn, what did he say? -- high stress reaction?

March 2

Brother phoned and said, "Your employers thought you would cave, give up. They miscalculated you; you are tough. We were brought up as pacifists with no violence. I believe that hard work and honesty gets rewarded."

March 7

MAKING A STAND FOR JUSTICE

Friend said, "Good, it's about time you got mad – you've been nice TOO long!"

In a conversation with Boss, I said, " I do not have a problem going to a doctor. I am stronger now than I was. The precedent has been set that violence in the workplace is acceptable behaviour. Do you know what it's like? Truckers put their fist by my face and say their load is dry wood. They gave me a club with Slugger's name on it. The truckers are being sarcastic because Slugger received no repercussions and they are on my side."

Boss' answer was, "You could have stayed at Needles if you didn't mind being there with Slugger. It was your choice."

I asked, "Do you believe I was hit?"

Boss: "I know something happened."

I asked if he knew where I was hit and Boss stuttered, "Well, I don't know..uh…the doctor's report said you were hit in..uh.. the ..uh…"

To my query about the police report, Boss replied, " I don't remember. Maybe ..uh..in the side of your..um..head."

Months of my frustration boiled out. 'Do you know why I wanted the ticket exchange on the railing? Because it was a simple solution to having no contact with Slugger. I have never been hit before and maybe this is a normal reaction to being hit to take some control. People tell me I should demand Slugger be fired and removed from my worksite, but no one would listen to me if I asked for that but I did want employers to show some support for me.'

Boss appeared to be listening. He said, "I understand now. Slugger does not say a word when he's in the scale shacks now. Having the loader-man in the scale shack when Slugger weighs in or doing a paper exchange on the railing with no contact is not normal work procedure."

I countered with, 'You said Slugger would not like those options, but assaulting is not normal work procedure.'

Boss confessed, "Maybe the Company Manager is afraid to do anything in case Slugger sues."

I mentioned another outstanding issue from October restricting me from contacting any personnel after hours. Seagull had said I wouldn't have insomnia if I had a young hunk in my bed. I wanted that rescinded. I stressed that Slugger was not just a danger to me, so I had warned other scalers. I tried to explain how incredibly hard I was hit. My counselor attributed my amnesia to the concussion.

In frustration, I added, "You have seen me once in six months."

MARCH 8
PROPOSED RESTRICTED CONTACT SCALE PROCEDURE

Snag Bay. 6th month anniversary present from Nor!!!!

He went to bat for me. He came to Snag Bay and drew up a procedure for Slugger having a paper exchange with no contact at the scales. Slugger remains in truck for remainder of time. I said, "It'll help, not just me, but everyone." Finally, recognition that I was assaulted. I am so happy!!!!

Nor said it's gone on too long with nothing done.

With Nor in the scale shack, a driver said, "Be quiet or I'll smack you."

March 14

Slugger approached two truckers on the ferry at 3:30 am and asked if they would back him because he should not be segregated (stay in truck at scales). If he has to, everyone should.

Nor brought a copy of 'Restricted Contact Scale Procedures' (RCSP) to Snag Bay.

Nor met with Slugger and his employers at which time Slugger said he didn't know about the letter. But – he told other drivers before he saw Nor!!

Slugger refused to sign RCSP and is going to a lawyer.

By having this agreement signed, I can then enforce it and have valid reason to report if Slugger, say, tries to enter scale shack. Finally!!! Concerns about health and safety are met. It is employers' obligation to do so. It has to make Nor and Company Manager happy to do something instead of burying their heads in sand. This form/procedure can be used for any future incidents within the Company.

I told Nor he could read my WorkSafe file if he wanted to verify I was violently assaulted.

March 19
FIT TO WORK

I got a letter from WorkSafe case manager. 'I do not require any other documentation regarding your fitness to return to work. Your employer may request some medical evidence to support your return to your previous work location, but I do not require this confirmation.'

So, what was all that from Boss saying WorkSafe case manager demanded doctor approval? Lie.

March 19
SNAG BAY CLOSURE

This is the last day for hauling to Snag Bay. Sort-yard will be cleaned out tomorrow.

I am forever thankful that WorkSafe backed me or where would I be now? A nut house? Or worse?

March 21
MEDICAL APPROVAL NEEDS SAFETY CONCERNS MET

Doctor appointment. Doctor wondered why he was being caught up in the middle of this. He said the neuro-psychologist would be better to decide if I am fit to work at Needles. He suggested it's more a lawyer issue. I explained that if I don't get a note stating I'm okay, then Boss will say I can't work at Needles. My doctor sees I am strong mentally and physically. I left him a letter from Boss saying the WorkSafe case manager needs approval, and also the letter from WorkSafe confirming they have no reason to ask for a medical.

March 29
FIRST AID EXPIRES

Boss phoned to say I start work at Needles on Monday.

I said I don't have medical approval yet. I showed my doctor your letter 'quoting' WorkSafe and mine from WorkSafe saying they would have no reason to ask for a medical. He is involving WorkSafe because it appears safety concerns are not being met.

Boss: 'I will phone and vouch for you.'

I replied, "I will see if I can visit the neuro-psychologist on Monday in Nelson.

I can only work for 2 weeks –my first aid ticket expires. I booked into May 5 course in January – it is the only course offered."

Boss: If it's only for a few weeks, it's okay.

Me: I checked if Worksafe would give me an extension and they said, "No."

Boss: I will check with Company Manager. You have so much experience.

Me: Then I would be working with no first aid certificate.

KEEP BAD PRACTICES SILENT

I didn't dare mention an uncertified, but assigned, Renata first aider; the company suppressed those incidents.

A trucker was hit in the head by an airborne chunk of log when dumping his load in the lake. The first aid attendant/scaler offered no care. The victim was disoriented, not knowing if he was weighing his truck in loaded or empty. Truckers arriving at the scales called the logging first aid attendant who got him to the hospital.

A second accident was also a head injury. A self-loading logging truck driver lowered the stabilizer legs so he could load his trailer. The loader-man was not in the clear and was struck in the head. The unqualified first aid attendant told the loader-man to drive himself to a hospital three hours away.

Re me: I am laughing and working long hours at home. Lots of energy. Nor helping me is so huge. Finally, my employers have come through. It should have happened 6 months ago but better late than never!

March 29

SAFETY CONCERNS NOT MET

I phoned neuro-psychologist's office, but he is booked until May. Neuro-psychologist said, "It was a bad enough ordeal without not having support and recognition from employers."

I want my job back. It's been 2 – 4 hours of travel a day. Now Needles is night shift, and no one wants it. Finally, after 6 months, a forester has helped me with restricted contact although Slugger refuses to sign it. I have been fighting for half a year – not just for me but also against violence, for all employees.

Boss said he will phone Worksafe, ask them to forget about doctor referral. I said, "I don't think they can; now there is a letter from my doctor referring me to WorkSafe and neuro-psychologist over safety concerns not being met."

Boss: There were no policies in place when I wrote the letter to you. So there should be no problem now.

I phoned WorkSafe and explained how my employer was pressuring me to return to Needles scales.

WorkSafe: But he was trying to keep you away.

Me: I know, but I have waited for six months, should I jeopardize everything by returning to work before the doctor assessment?

WorkSafe: We should have all our ducks in a row, and I suggest you not return to work until the neuro-psychologist's assessment is done.

Me: I told Boss my first aid is going to expire, and he said I had lots of experience and it should be okay to work as a first aid attendant without it.

Worksafe: He's not looking out for you and you could be in trouble.

Me: ..and he could be in trouble.

NOW BOSS WANTS ME AT NEEDLES??

WorkSafe called me:

WorkSafe just got off the phone with Boss. Boss talked about Restricted Contact Scale Procedure and said Slugger will have to stay away until he signs. Boss wants me at work a.s.a.p. and still wants me to go to neuro-psychologist but it could be done later.

Needles is on night shift with 3:30 a.m. start and other scalers do not want to work. My first aid runs out April 16.

Boss: It is okay to work after your first aid expires. The Company has given permission before to people as long as they are booked in for a course.

Me: I phoned WorkSafe in Richmond and they said there are no extensions.

April 3

MY OWN SAFETY PLAN WITH NO EMPLOYER SUPPORT

I had a phone call with the neuro-psychologist:

WorkSafe asked him a specific question: 'Is the doctor opposed to me working at Needles?'

I told him Slugger's truck wasn't being insured.

Doctor: That's just a HOPE Slugger won't be there. Your employers have promised before and I do not have a letter confirming anything. From history, Slugger could return. Employer has not been supportive, possibly will not be supportive in the future. Reality predicts the past will repeat itself in the future. Send me: 1. What plans are in place? 2. What you would do if the trucker showed up? 3. What do you think is reasonable for a start date?

I suggest you go in on your own time with another scaler present. I am concerned they will use my remarks to their advantage. For example, my suggesting employing you at scales not used by trucker; why didn't they remove the trucker?

The issue is the person, not the truck. Slugger could show up in a different truck. I will call WorkSafe's psychologist. Hold off for a bit, some issues need to be resolved. What would you do if Slugger showed up? How would you handle it?

Me: Call a loader-man.

Doctor: Have your employers talked to the loader-man about being present when Slugger is at the scales?

Me: No, they said they would, but I don't think they have at this time. I have to be strong about returning or I will be sent to Renata – four hours travel per day.

Doctor: Your employers told you before that Slugger wouldn't show up and he did…why do you trust what they say?

PREPARING MY OWN SAFETY PLAN

I stayed up late writing a letter to the neuro-psychologist to confirm that I have my own safety plan for violence and threats, knowing I have no support from my employers. I have a phone. I can close scale door. I can lock myself in my truck. I have bear spray and a tape recorder. I can radio for help or even hold the mike button on to broadcast verbal threats.

Why are my employers refusing to acknowledge the assault? Being sucker-punched while I signed a weigh slip should not be acceptable behaviour.

April 24
NO RESTRICTED SCALE PROCEDURE…YET

Neuro-psychologist told WorkSafe that the labor issue is not settled, i.e. the trucker refused to sign a restricted contact order. WorkSafe deals with injury and doesn't get involved with labor issues.

I called Company Manager to ask what procedures regarding Slugger at the scales have been implemented.

Company Manager said. "No change. The intent is to get Slugger to sign the Restricted Scale Contact procedure, but it is not in place. If Slugger doesn't sign, I am not sure what I will do."

How am I doing? Well, I have not been so close to tears for a lot of months. After phone calls this morning, I am so frustrated.

Many friends figure it's time for a lawyer. Everything is going around and around in circles.

April 25
LABOUR ISSUE ALSO SAFETY ISSUE

Neuro-psychologist called. He said it is unlikely in his opinion that my employers will do anything. (The trucker is not signing Restricted Contact Procedure.)

He asked me general questions (nightmares? Startle easily?). I said I was good for one and a half months after Nor started to take action by initiating a no contact procedure. Yesterday, I was upset and frustrated. He said those were normal emotions.

I asked, "Why is WorkSafe involved if this is a labor issue?"

The neuro-psychologist replied, "Labor relations is a conflict between employer and employee and Worksafe does not get involved. In your case, the conflict between employer and employee relates to your safety."

April 26

NO-CONTACT SAFETY PLAN ABANDONED

Boss said he was sending me a letter from the Company Manager.

I asked, "What's in the letter; what did the Company Manager say?"

Boss: Uh, uh…railing thing is out (for no contact paper exchange)…uh..get loader-man..

Me: Seagull suggested that way back, but it will not work. How can a loader-man be at the scales if he is dumping five trucks at the time?

Boss: Oh, well. You could have a meeting with the Company Manager.

Me: I will go and see him. I've been the one paying – my assailant got nothing.

I was told after the September 14 meeting that there were two stories, and no one wanted to take sides. I sent the Company Manager my WorkSafe file to prove I was hit and requested the decision be revisited but his reply was, "We never made a decision."

Boss: I appealed to WorkSafe over the bill. Unfair that I got a bill for something Slugger caused…I am very bothered by that.

Me: Slugger hit me at work, but it was no accident. I hope you win because if Slugger's employer gets a bill, he will take it out of Slugger's hide.

Boss: I never thought of that.

FIT TO RETURN TO WORK

WorkSafe will be doing a closure letter to me, copy to Boss. I am fit to return to work, any location. No limitation. The safety plan in place is my personal plan: phone, radio, lock door etc.

Boss is required to do monthly safety meetings but has not been. He saw me one time. Employers can still do something. Violence is not acceptable.'

I thought Nor told me if Slugger didn't sign, he would be told he couldn't haul to my scales?

A friend said, "Now Slugger has been given the power, he certainly will power trip on you again. Maybe just verbally, but…."

MAY 7
NEEDLES SCALES

Needles!!!!

Boss set up computers. Went over safety program. All this is just so much paper if it isn't followed. Boss said Slugger did admit to touching me and there were grounds to deal with inappropriate touching, but Slugger didn't get so much as a disciplinary letter.

After Boss left, a Vernon trucker was told, by locals over the radio, "If Lois gives you any lip, local boys know how to deal with her." A joke but I am not laughing.

May 14
WORKSAFE REVIEW IN MY FAVOUR

A Company forester asked, "What are you going to do when Slugger shows up?"

I said the psychologist was satisfied with my personal plan and said I would be prepared for him this time."

I got Request for Review results from WorkSafe. They ruled in my favour, not Boss'. No surprise to me. (Results are available on-line: www.Worksafebc.com request for review #R074710.) This is the third time Boss has tried to get my claim denied while seeing me one time within six months of the assault.

Boss phoned and said, "I lack communication skills. I flip-flop. I should have communicated better. I read the doctors' reports, did some reading, now I believe you were hit."

I asked, "Did you ever go to Company Manager regarding Seagull's comments to me in October resulting in that I cannot call personnel after hours? It really bothers me, especially since Seagull has retired."

Boss replied, "No, I forgot."

May 15
RENATA SEEMS TO BE PLANNED FOR ME

Seemore said Boss approached him re. taking me to Renata this year. Seemore refused to take me because he works late and it's not fair for me to wait and he added, "Put Red or Baby there." Those scalers historically camped and enjoyed Renata.

Boss said, "I don't like them there alone at night."

Seemore replied, "There are always lots of people there."

Boss retorted, "Baby needs a place to work. If Lois was at Renata, Baby could have Needles."

June 4
PLEASE RESCIND OCTOBER RESTRICTION

Needles reopened.

Boss said I could call company employees at home after hours if there is no answer on the radio.

I replied, "The letter from October prohibiting that is still in effect." Boss wrote a note on his hand because he said he keeps forgetting about that.

I painted the back and sides of a balsam load and Boss challenged me on that. I said that is approved policy for years after truckers complained about paint spraying on their trucks. Boss couldn't contain his glee at catching me at something. I never pointed out that painting any balsam load was totally redundant since balsam is now 100% sorted. Tug-boaters don't have to wonder if a load is 60% balsam or 60% spruce.

June 7
LOSING HOPE, GAINING DESPAIR

Boss smugly delivered a disciplinary letter saying the new Company Manager definitely did not approve of my not painting the front of balsam loads. It is apparent to me that 'violations' of any sort, or even fabrications, were to be used to terminate me. Why?

June 29

DELIBERATE COMPANY SILENCE

A company employee brought scaling supplies. He said the whole thing (assault) was hush, hush and never even mentioned at safety meetings.

July 6

Took day off. Two scalers worked that day. That is usual when I am absent.

July 10

Frank (loader-man) wants me to have help Wednesday. The yard truck will be here Thursday. Left message with Boss but he never returns my calls.

July 27

The forest fire by Whatshan powerline is raging. Ash is falling on the sort-yard. Hottest July on record.

Phoned Boss to give my hours worked. He asked how things were going. Slower?

I said, "I did 5 samples in the last 2 days and have 1 big hemlock load to scale."

Boss asked, "What?"

I repeated it.

Boss said, "It's hot outside. Well done."

September 10

Boss and Baby here from 8:30 – 11:15 but they left samples unscaled that Lars had already spread.

I asked Boss if they were going to do them and he said, "No, we have other places to go and work." He knew I wasn't getting a break between trucks.

September 20

RENATA SCALE TRANSFER OR FIRED.

Boss and Baby show up at Needles scales. Boss said if I don't go to Renata, I will be fired.

I had an emotional time. I was crying.

A friend said after, "That's PTSD." Definitely like rug pulled out from under my feet.

There were samples spread to scale. They did none. Boss was really upset over seeing a tape recorder on my desk. I said, "There is a tape recorder, camera and bear spray in case Slugger shows up."

Boss replied, "I should learn to ask questions instead of getting upset."

September 25

COMMUTING TO RENATA - PRIOR TO LIVING THERE?

Boss said Seemore was planning on camping in Renata. Boss arranged for room and board for me at Renata. My accommodation would be a camper. I asked Boss what I needed to stay there? Bedding, cutlery, crockery? Is there a fridge, stove, water, toilet facilities? Boss said he didn't know.

I traveled with the loader-man to Renata Monday and Tuesday. Big joke between a trucker and regular Renata scaler what I was expected to live in.

September 27

When I called to give my hours worked, Boss said I would have to take propane to Renata and asked if I had propane tanks.

I replied, "I do not have propane tanks. I was told the camper had no road access so I did not know how I could even get propane tanks there."

Boss stated, "The Company Manager asked if you are interested in a meeting regarding the assault."

I replied, "Yes, I've wanted that for a year."

OCTOBER 1
RENATA

Seemore said Jorge and Glory sold their place and are living in the camper that I was to use, and Boss had been told the rental was available only for last week.

October 2

Nor came to Renata.

Nor assertively declared, "The logging contractors that Slugger hauls from may be coming to work in Renata. How did you feel about having Slugger haul here? Can you deal with it? Maybe the truckers can help you."

I felt gut-punched and replied, "I had to satisfy the neuro-psychologist that I would be okay at Needles."

Nor reproached, "Why do you want to live in Edgewood anyways? Why don't you get a new career, maybe with the Forest Service?"

When Nor left, I walked along the beach. Seemore thought I was coming to see him, so he stopped the loader. I was crying from Nor's hurtful comments.

Seemore noticed I have changed: no laughter, no joy. What happened to the restricted contact procedure? Deal with Slugger yourself.

Have my employers set the precedent that violence in the workplace is acceptable behaviour? The effects of the assault will be with me for the rest of my life. I now struggle to survive.

October 3
TOUGHER TO REBOUND

Seemore commented, "Everyone knows you were hit but they want it to go away."

I said, "I was told I could have a meeting with the Company and I want it. I can stick to:

1. I was hit.

2. What are you going to do?"

This has been the toughest year of my life. I just start getting on my feet and they knock me down again. Again and again. It's getting tougher to rebound. I expect a counselor will only offer the usual sympathy and disbelief at the deplorable treatment by my employers.

Is history repeating itself? When Manly reported dishonest scaling (which Boss admitted to knowing of), Manly was laid off. He was removed to scales he had never worked at and told he could not go back to his regular scales.

It began with an assault, but the bad treatment did not end there. It's what has happened <u>subsequent</u> to the attack that hurt me the most.

OCTOBER 5
WORD THAT I AM HISTORY

Phone message quite late last night from Boss: "Dump the first round of trucks, clean up samples, bring in power cords etc. with computer." This was to be my last day of employment.

Boss: 'I am replacing you at Renata because I need the money.' Renata is the farthest distance from his home in Nakusp, 6 hours travel/day. The other scales and mill sites are closer. Records prove he seldom took a steady position at scales.

He would travel from Edgewood with the loader-man. The usual Renata scaler residing in Nelson would work at Boss' usual job at a millsite in Nakusp.

December 16
WHY? WHY?

Other scalers worked after my lay-off; three at Octopus scales. Seemore said Renata scales are still open.

I wonder why I had delusions of fair treatment with justice and truth eventually winning. It's awful. I am so messed up mentally and not happy. Tormented days and sleepless nights. Nightly I lie awake with my mind spinning with, 'Why? Why don't they believe me? I am not a liar."

I have nightmares: Slugger in front of me laughing and Boss watching and laughing.

Last week, I wrote Boss requesting my promised meeting with the Company and Slugger's employers. A friend is willing to go with me, but he figures there will never be a meeting arranged.

January 9
I GET A COMPANY MEETING

Phone message from Boss – meeting 4:30 pm January 14 at Company office.

January 14

Today is my meeting at the Company office. I am so thankful I prepared my statements. I added an impact statement, writing it at 3:00 a.m. with pen and ink and no errors. Then I slept.

I was not sure if I would be allowed to speak or if they would say, "Too late. Go away."

MY FIRST MEETING WITH EMPLOYERS AND SLUGGER'S' EMPLOYERS

JANUARY 14 – My presentation:

> Thank you for arranging this meeting. This is very important to me. I was deliberately struck in the face by a co-worker. I suffered two traumas: firstly the assault, but secondly post-traumatic stress disorder that could have been prevented if employers had obeyed labor laws. THE ASSAULT WAS NOT PREVENTABLE BUT THE PROCEDURES FOLLOWING THE INCIDENT WERE CRITICAL. Negative effects of P.T.S.D. will remain for the rest of my life.
>
> In reviewing the actions taken to rectify the situation, it appears that being struck by a co-worker was deemed

acceptable behaviour. I WAS DELIBERATELY STRUCK IN THE FACE WITH ENOUGH FORCE TO LOSE CONSCIOUSNESS. Why then am I still fighting for my legal rights <u>sixteen months later?</u>

1. I want recognition from employers that I am a victim of assault and battery in the workplace and that I have suffered greatly although much was preventable.

    B.C. Occupational Health and Safety Regulations state I should have been immediately referred to a doctor, counselor, and R.C.M.P. The incident should have been immediately reported to WorkSafe. I was entitled to a meeting with all parties present and an investigation.

    Company policies say, in regard to victims of physical contact, 'the supervisor is responsible to confirm the facts and meet with the individuals involved to attain a solution to the situation and ensure the offensive conduct will not be repeated. When an offended individual is not satisfied with the resolution achieved, the Supervisor and the individual will review with the Superintendent, Manager or Human Resources Supervisor.

    The above were not done.

    Further policies say, 'incidences of…violence shall be reported, investigated and documented'.

    My immediate employer saw me once in the six months following the incident; that was three months after.

    I submitted reports to employers, as evidence I was struck in the face by the assailant, from R.C.M.P., Crown Prosecutor, two doctors, counselor, psychiatrist, WorkSafe and neuro-psychologist. Crown Counsel said there was no doubt I had been hit. My initial visit to the neuro-psychologist was three months after the incident yet his diagnosis was that I was not fully recovered. I asked that the company's decision, that there were two stories and they did not want to take sides, be revisited. I was told that a decision had not been made. These are crimes recognized by the criminal justice system so why are they not even being recognized as workplace violations?

The second assault that day was verbal: being told I was lucky I called his load dry or I'd be extricating his boot from my asshole. The assailant did say he patted me, which is inappropriate workplace behaviour (although it was a blow, not a pat).

The criminal assault and battery in the workplace has not even inconvenienced the perpetrator while I have lost in many respects due in large part to protocols not being met.

2. I want safety policies in the workplace to ensure protection and support in regards to violence.

    Any person who is violent in the workplace is a danger. Workers have the right to refuse unsafe work conditions.

    A gradual return to work was recommended by WorkSafe and doctors but was not supported by employers. I had to satisfy the neuro-psychologist and WorkSafe that I was capable of facing my attacker on my worksite with no support from employers. I was ordered off work by my doctor; I initiated my return. I was commended by doctors and WorkSafe for my personal drive in returning to work and health so quickly. That is a credit to my strengths and commitment.

3. I want the violator held accountable for his actions.

    A man with a volatile temper grievously attacked a co-worker. Nothing has been done to remove or even mitigate this workplace hazard.

    B.C. Occupational, Health and Safety regulations: 'An employer must inform workers who may be exposed to the risk of violence of the nature and extent of the risk. That...includes a duty to provide information related to the risk of violence from persons who have a history of violent behaviour and whom workers are likely to encounter in the course of their work.'

Company policy states: 'Disciplinary action: Individuals will be accountable for their behaviour. Depending on the severity and repetitiveness of the conduct, appropriate discipline may be: -written warning to the individual's file, suspension from active employment, termination for cause.'

4. I want no retributions against me or loss of work for filing a complaint on physical violence or receiving a WorkSafe claim.

A company employee suggested I move away and find another career because my assailant was expected to work at my job site and the company was offering me no support. I should not be driven from my job. I was removed from my worksite so the assailant could remain there. I was told he was compensated for a longer haul when a court order denied him access to the usual site. When I was relocated, I had up to four hours unpaid travel per day.

5. I want you to make amends and correct misjudgments. I want justice, not just for me, but for everyone.

My co-workers are aware that there were no repercussions for a person attacking a co-worker and that labour laws were ignored. Workers cannot feel safe when you are not prepared to protect them.

ATTACHMENTS:

I am submitting a witness statement and my comments in regard to the meeting held after the violent assault on September 14. Slugger was invited to speak; his statements were supposedly made in the presence of a third person (Lars) the company never interviewed.

IMPACT STATEMENT
PRESENTED TO EMPLOYERS AND SLUGGER'S EMPLOYERS
January 14

If I broke my leg at work, you would not deny me treatment or question why I could not work. A broken leg would have healed a year ago. I did not have a broken leg, I had head and brain trauma and I am not yet healed.

You walk without appreciating your legs' ability to carry you; so we take our brains for granted. Knowing how to make a cup of tea, my memory, coherent talk and ability to read a book were all taken away from me after the assault. I had no physical strength. I could not remember to eat. I had severe insomnia. I had fears of being attacked. PTSD is totally debilitating.

If it'd been a broken leg, would my employer have been upset I filed a WorkSafe claim, made objections to my claim being accepted and then asked for a review of my claim once it was final?

It is easy to understand why you can't walk with a broken leg and how it can be treated. It is not easy to understand the loss of mental powers and how to fix it. Brains do not break or heal like a broken bone. One employee (*workplace head injury*) is a staunch ally because he understands the struggles and challenges I have endured.

I was positively euphoric when a restricted contact scale procedure was proposed. (*Slugger would remain in his truck and avoid contact with me while on the scales.*)

IT WAS THE FIRST SUPPORT OFFERED ME BY YOU!! THE PHYSICAL ASSAULT IN THE WORKPLACE WAS BEING ACKNOWLEDGED!!!

A trucker's reaction to my joy was to say, "Slugger should have been fired."

My neuro-psychologist's comment was, "They've lied to you before; what makes you think they aren't lying to you again?" That set me down with a bump but the restricted contact scale procedure was never enacted. Now I am happy to finally get my meeting. Do I dare hope?

I cannot just get over a broken leg if I am left laying in the sort-yard with no treatment.

If a hole in the scale deck caused my broken leg, would you fix the hole? I need your help to heal my injuries. To hope the whole incident will just quietly go away, is like leaving me lie in the sort-yard while gangrene takes my life, so the broken leg and hole don't have to be dealt with.

At work, I often felt like I was trying to walk with two broken legs with no one offering a hand. I could only crawl during those tough times, but I kept moving. I was knocked down repeatedly but not defeated. COURAGE IS THE MASTERY OF FEAR. Can you appreciate how much fear I had to master to have enough courage to believe I could face my attacker on my worksite with no support from you? I was cold cocked at my desk with an unimaginable amount of force. There was no warning, no provocation and no admission of guilt by 'Slugger' for his actions. He is fully aware of the seriousness of his actions. He was permitted the privilege of unchallenged statements and unpunished behaviour in the workplace. He lawyered up and said nothing to the R.C.M.P.; he knows the seriousness of the crime and he knows how the legal system works. He must have known I was unconscious but has shown no remorse – his #1 concern was to run and save his ass.

I have watched TV – I thought the violator would have to swear in court to tell the truth, and would be questioned on the stand and truth (I) would win. Real life means a violator never has to get on the stand to be questioned but the Crown must prove beyond all reasonable doubt the crime happened. The Crown prosecutor told me she knows I was hit.

She acknowledges that it is a heinous crime and that he is likely to re-offend. It did not proceed to criminal court because 'Slugger' and I were not arguing, no reason for them to present why he hit me but if his load had been stratified as 'green', there would have been 'cause'. There also were no direct witnesses.

I allege I am the second female scaler *(from the same scaling company)* to be punched in the face by 'Slugger' so I hope my fight for justice prevents more. Don't his actions raise a red flag? He put the weigh slip on the desk and deliberately hit me while I was looking down at my desk. The loader-man said 'Slugger' was agitated when he weighed in, possibly from school issues, was it uncontrollable anger from that? Consider that I never regained consciousness to find him hovering over me, concerned he hurt me. So far, it appears you condoned his behavior. That hurts. An apology from 'Slugger' will place him in jail; he knows running from the assault and some smooth talking has gotten him out of even workplace repercussions. So far. YOU STILL CAN AND SHOULD HOLD THE VIOLATOR ACCOUNTABLE FOR HIS ACTIONS. You have the power!

Can you appreciate my personal triumph when I conquered Needles – the busy and difficult scales? I was as proud as if I had climbed Mount Everest solo. It wasn't long before that I didn't know how to make a cup of tea. My counselor told me some people could have taken a year to achieve what I did in two months.

I did not have an accident and break my leg. My injuries were man-caused. Knowing my life has changed irreversibly, because of deliberate and preventable causes, weighs on me constantly. I need your help to complete my healing; I cannot simply 'get over it' because I do face a lifetime of effects of post-traumatic stress disorder. You have the power to change current negative effects to positive effects. In the process, I believe you will receive positive personal returns. I do not believe you lack compassion or a sense of justice and you then must be carrying personal burdens knowing I was wronged. If we had both taken the easy roads, this incident would have been quietly passed by and I would have allowed myself to be defeated. This is not just about me, it's about ignored labour laws and rights that affect everyone everywhere: I was violently assaulted while sitting at my desk and my employers have not supported me. Policies and regulations are just so much paper if they are not enforced.

I chose the right road, the hard road. It has been four-wheel drive and rough but I am hoping it smooths out around the next corner. If you detour from the easy road, and join me on the right road, the one heading toward justice, we can all work toward a happy ending.

I RECEIVED NO RESPONSE AFTER THIS MEETING.

A friend accompanying me told those at the meeting that he witnessed Slugger harassing other scalers.

Nor suggested a barrier to define scalers' work areas. Boss sat at the far end of the board table, away from everyone, with his head down. I remember he only said that HE didn't need a defined work area at HIS scales. That upset me. It implied Slugger would have only hit me, yet he had hit another female scaling employee in the face.

Later, I would learn Slugger physically and verbally assaulted logging contractors prior to the violence against me. Usually, they had simply banned Slugger from hauling from their sites and not reported the cases. My incident was intentionally silenced; most were unaware of the violence against me. Would documented history of Slugger's behavior have altered the companies' responses?

All my pleas to present the truth have been ignored. Why?

Was how to care for employees after a violent attack, prevention and understanding of critical incidence stress and P.T.S.D. learned and understood?

My employers seemed to pretend nothing happened. Violence in the workplace was deemed acceptable behaviour; just remove the victim.

So ended my cherished career as a log scaler.

This is my depiction of a violent attack and the decision made by my employers to negate it.

PART 3
Searching for Truth and Justice

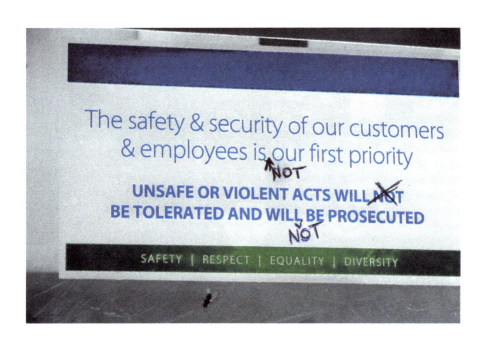

SEARCHING FOR TRUTH AND JUSTICE

GOVERNMENT OFFERED FUNDING FOR WORKERS TO EXIT FORESTRY

A government program offered funding for forestry workers wishing to transition out of the forestry field. An option was to work for six months after approval of their application. In my case, I had been laid off a year prior, but I did meet their criteria.

My preference would have been log scaling for at least ten more years but apparently I did not have that option at my former position. With only about 250 active licensed scalers in the B.C. interior (U.S.A. to Yukon), job opportunities were minimal.

The agency said I could continue to attempt recovering employment monies due me prior to the initiation of the program and my application. The only consequence might be repaying some of the amount received from my employer to the government program. To me, justice took priority over financial rewards.

PREPARING FOR COURT

Meeting a co-worker at a new direction in employment was a godsend. Deb was horrified when she heard of the violent assault and my subsequent termination. She offered her support to take action for wrongful dismissal.

Post- traumatic stress disorder was not solely from the assault; more devastating was post-assault treatment by my employers, including job termination.

I carried life-long negative effects. We agreed we wanted, not revenge, but truth and justice to enable me to heal.

Small Claims Court is for those with under $25,000 claims, without a lawyer and without liability for legal costs from the other party. Settlement hearings allow a judge to mediate both parties' concerns and ideally reach an agreement to avoid a trial.

A mixed-up box of papers grew into a comprehensive study of appropriate laws, case laws giving examples of successful settlements and documents to support my claim for wrongful dismissal and severance pay from log scaling. My confidence grew with an understanding of laws and the organized document file supporting my case.

TRUTH AND JUSTICE FINALLY HAPPEN?
FIRST SETTLEMENT CONFERENCE

At the first settlement conference, I explained my legal case for wrongful dismissal. The judge requested more details. The months of preparation all seemed so worthwhile as the judge listened intently and sympathetically.

Judge F ordered that a public apology for me was to be drawn up by my (ex) employers' (the Defendants') lawyer. The detailed statement was to be posted at all weigh scales.

My former employer agreed, "Yes, she was treated wrongly, and I will give her scaling job back."

At this, months of pain dissolved into an emotional release full of tears. Finally, the code of deliberate silence over the violent assault would be broken.

The judge asked me to meet with him outside the courtroom where I received an unexpected hug and heartfelt words of encouragement for the positive resolution. My case went beyond the legal case to compassion for the dreadful experiences I had related. Even ex-Boss surprised Deb and me with hugs and saying he was sorry.

THE SECOND SETTLEMENT HEARING

Judge F opened the meeting stating, "The last meeting was a decision to present a cash offer, job offer and an apology.

The Defendant stated, "I am withdrawing my offer to re-employ Ms. Wood and the apology." The judge did not intend, and stated so, for the Defendant to demand a large payment from me for the apology prior to this meeting. That apology stated I had been assaulted and admitted negligence for the employers' actions and lack of. Perhaps that went beyond their 'comfort zone'.

I stated, "A sincere apology does not come with a price tag and I did not pay the Defendant for the apology."

Why did the judge not enforce his order for a public apology? How is it that agreements made in Court can be withdrawn? So began my misgivings of Court.

A signed offer to settle for $12,000 was agreed upon by both parties.

THE THIRD SETTLEMENT HEARING

Why was the signed $12,000 agreement negated? Judge S asked my former employer, and his lawyer, if they were willing to make an offer to settle the claim. Their offer was $200, which I declined.

I fearlessly replied, "Then I wish to proceed to trial. A wound does not heal unless you let the pus and poison out."

TRIAL

Trial began with Judge M at the bench.

As a consequence of PTSD, I was commonly unable to hold a train of thought for more than five minutes. My thoughts would drift, and I wondered, "What was I talking about?"

I was on the witness stand for about four hours and never faltered. Because of my pivotal part in researching the laws, collecting the evidence and organizing the documents, I felt strong, determined and prepared to present the facts relevant to being wrongfully dismissed from my log scaling profession.

The newfound strength is likely lifelong.

Court was not what I anticipated. Why had I expected Court etiquette and respect for a higher authority of justice?

Documents materialized from the defendant's lawyer. If this was an attempt to intimidate me, it did not.

Many were entered as evidence (exhibits) and are publicly available with the Court transcript. Wood v Pattom, Nakusp court # 1139.

I received different versions of documents I had previously submitted through the Court document disclosure package and alleged copies of letters new to me. How many times would this be repeated? Ten? Fifteen? I became leery of touching the mail in case I smeared fresh ink.

I challenged (ex) Boss' payroll records submitted as evidence, based on the Harvest Billing System records available on-line from the B.C. Government. These display all scaling dates, locations, load information and scalers.

The Judge was openly disturbed to hear my former employers' submitted payroll records were not accurate. The Defendant's explanation was that employees' names were not required when billing the timber company.

One memorable excuse to lower my seniority ranking was Boss stating his son was a senior employee to me when he helped daddy by holding a measuring tape as a young teenager, without a scaling license and likely not on payroll.

The lawyer entered a defense that my monetary success in Court may have to be repaid to the program funding for laid off forestry workers.

The Judge clearly responded, "That is not a concern of the Court."

By not producing an argument, the Defendant agreed I was not dismissed with cause, that I never refused employment, that I was a victim of a violent assault and that I never quit my employment. After their extensive communication with the government funding agency, no mention of improprieties were noted.

In the judge's decision, she confirmed I had been knocked unconscious in an assault and that I had been wrongfully dismissed with three separate incidents. She said I was not entitled to severance pay because I had not received it previously.

She interpreted the government sponsored funding program contrary to the agency's advice to me and their correspondence in my document disclosure.

I was not awarded financial compensation. I did not receive the judge ordered apology, the signed agreement for $12,000 or the job offer.

FINANCIAL PENALTY

Judge M ordered a payment hearing to assign a financial penalty for me allegedly taking a case to court with no reasonable chance of success. The lawyer I consulted was opposed to the judge's decision. He prepared case laws and legal advice for me to present.

In the Courtroom, the judge was receptive to the Defendant's claim for an unknown number of photocopies and other undocumented costs.

I thought I could respond but Judge M refused to allow me to speak.

Annoyed, she said, "You should have a lawyer."

As I began to counter with, "I do have a lawyer…," the judge gathered up her papers and left the Courtroom. I was effectively dismissed and unable to present statements prepared by my attorney.

IS THIS A LOSS OR A WIN?

I was ordered to pay a penalty. This is not justice.

I did gain personal strength and I do not regret trying.

I learned justice couldn't exist without truth. I lost belief in equity and lawful rights.

IN SUMMARY

I know the importance of accurate scaling. My honesty, accuracy and diligence are apparent in my journals. I am proud of my achievements as a log scaler.

Sadly, my employers chose to approve of violence in their worksite, to my detriment. Why, when they knew I was harmed, did they not rectify some of the damage and admit they had erred? Why not weeks later? Months later?

Compassion with legal and moral responsibilities must come ahead of financial considerations. The hours my employers spent fighting against fair treatment would have been better spent in efforts to achieve it.

The hardships I endured are tragically commonplace, unnecessary and in contravention of workplace policies and procedures.

I have met many employees fired for reporting violence, safety issues or hazards. How many more will die because fear of losing their job overcomes the right of reporting dangers or injuries?

I was driven to present my story on behalf of all who have been suppressed.

I will not be silenced, and I will continue to make a stand against injustices.

To think a small voice cannot be heard, simply think of a mosquito in a darkened bedroom.

The important things in life are not 'things'.

CPSIA information can be obtained
at www.ICGtesting.com
Printed in the USA
BVHW020728290621
610332BV00005B/5